What people are saying about
Samuel Betances'
Ten Steps to the Head of the Class:
A Challenge to Students

"Long overdue... Dr. Betances' approach is essential to students who are not reaching their potential in America's schools. Students can easily evaluate their own learner behaviors and now have access to strategies that will greatly improve their own personal efficacy."

Dr. George Sisemore, Director, Professional Center for School Conferences
Phoenix, AZ

"Dr. Betances' book is both insightful and extremely helpful. It is a must read for any student who is serious about succeeding in academia. Where was this book when I was in school?"

Jacob Vargas, Actor
Van Nuys, CA

"I found the book to be very helpful as I prepare for college. I have been used to just doing what I have to do, and often at the last minute. Procrasti-cramming may help me get along for now, but I'm afraid that, in college, the bad habit might do me in."

Maria Noboa, High School Student
Granville, OH

"This book will serve as an inspiration to everyone who reads it. Whether you are trying to put yourself on the right track academically or organize your life, Dr. Betances shows you how to do it in a way that is both meaningful and interactive"

Ingrid Sanders, Journalism Student, University of Missouri-Columbia
Columbia, MO

"Samuel Betances does it again. This is a "must" read for those who want to move from academic mediocrity to excellence or for those who excel and want to inspire others to do the same."

Dr. Antonio R. Flores, President, Hispanic Association of Colleges and Universities
San Antonio, TX

"This book is for guidance and inspiration. It pinpoints specific problems that students have been having for years. Not only does this book give you tips on what to do, but it lets you know how to do it as well"

Gina Hampton, Adult Learning Skills Program Student, Olive-Harvey College
Chicago, IL

"Dr. Betances has done a terrific job of suggesting both practical and logical steps for students to follow in improving their own study habits. I am about to start an MBA program at Columbia University. Since I have been out of school for over ten years now, I read this book with great interest, and I am confident the tips recommended will help me as I pursue this degree. Again Dr. Betances is right on the mark!"

R. Gaynor McCown, Vice President of Corporate Strategies, The Edison Project
New York, NY

"I found this book to be exciting, provocative, challenging and utilitarian. The format is so "clean and clear." The concrete way you presented the information makes it a real "hands on" tool for kids. Hopefully the value of this book will b recognized by schools and organizations so that kids can be educated with it as they reflect on where they are and where they want to go."

Marge Tye Zuba, Ed.D, LCSW, International Educational Consultant, Author of Wish I Could Have Told You Chicago, IL

Dedication

For Dr. Robert B. Binswanger, my teacher,
mentor and friend.

Samuel Betances

Ten Steps
to The Head
of The Class

A Challenge
to Students

New Century Forum Inc.
Chicago

TEN STEPS TO THE HEAD OF THE CLASS:
A CHALLENGE TO STUDENTS

Printed in the United States of America

New Century Forum Inc.
6348 North Milwaukee Ave., PMB 319
Chicago, IL 60646-3728

ISBN 1-891438-02-6
Library of Congress Catalog Card Number: 99-66291

Table of Contents

Introduction   11
Step 1-Stop Procrasti-Cramming   19

    Lessons from the Literature   20
    You Be the Judge   21
    The Habit: Procrasti-Cramming   23
    My Personal Commitment   27
    Lasting Thoughts   29

Step 2-Stop Reckless Reading   31

    Lessons from the Literature   32
    You Be the Judge   33
    The Habit: Reckless Reading   35
    My Personal Commitment   39
    Lasting Thoughts   41

Step 3-Stop Fishing for Answers   43

    Lessons from the Literature   44
    You Be the Judge   45
    The Habit: Fishing for Answers   47
    My Personal Commitment   52
    Lasting Thoughts   54

Step 4-Stop Post-Lecture Reading   55

    Lessons from the Literature   56
    You Be the Judge   57
    The Habit: Post-Lecture Reading   59
    My Personal Commitment   64
    Lasting Thoughts   66

Step 5-Stop Loafing in the Place of Study   67

    Lessons from the Literature   68
    You Be the Judge   69
    The Habit: Loafing in the Place of Study   71
    My Personal Commitment   77
    Lasting Thoughts   79

Step 6-Stop Going Solo   **81**

Lessons from the Literature   82
You Be the Judge   83
The Habit: Going Solo   85
My Personal Commitment   91
Lasting Thoughts   93

Step 7-Stop Viewing Teachers as Adultists   **95**

Lessons from the Literature   96
You Be the Judge   97
The Habit: Viewing Teachers as Adultists   101
My Personal Commitment   111
Lasting Thoughts   113

Step 8-Stop Seeking Solutions without Education   **115**

Lessons from the Literature   116
You Be the Judge   117
The Habit: Seeking Solutions without Education   121
My Personal Commitment   128
Lasting Thoughts   130

Step 9-Stop Pursuing Logical Paths to Wrong Destinations   **133**

Lessons from the Literature   134
You Be the Judge   135
The Habit: Pursuing Logical Paths to Wrong Destinations   139
My Personal Commitment   147
Lasting Thoughts   149

Step 10-Stop Failing to Look Up by Not Getting Down   **151**

Lessons from the Literature   152
You Be the Judge   153
The Habit: Failing to Look Up by Not Getting Down   157
My Personal Commitment   162
Lasting Thoughts   164

Bibliography   **165**

Acknowledgments

I would like to express my most heartfelt appreciation to:

Dr. Laura Marie Torres Souder, my C.E.O., colleague, spouse and best friend, for her tireless work on my behalf and the success of this project.

Dr. David Quitugua who provided invaluable editorial assistance and spiritual guidance.

Dr. Rosita Marcano for her encouragement and passionate belief that the book is sorely needed.

Dr. Abdin Noboa for giving life to the component "You Be the Judge."

Don O'Shaughnessy and Tess Malolos of New Century Forum, Inc. for their superb assistance in all matters related to editorial and organizational presentation.

Our professional team at Souder, Betances and Associates, especially Shawn Surber, my Business Manager and brainstorming partner on shaping the vision and mission of each chapter.

Carlos Jimenez who researched the quotes for the "Lasting Thoughts" section.

David, my son, for the idea of "Going Solo" as a chapter.

Brian, Brittany, Michael, Erin, Eric and Mari, the cadre of students whose insightful feedback and practical recommendations challenged me to make each chapter short and fun to read.

My family on Guam, Hawaii, California, Puerto Rico and Chicago whose prayers, love and moral support continue to give me strength to pursue my dreams and aspirations.

Ilya and Vesna Vasilj for making their home an oasis for loving, spirited discussions on education and parenting.

Introduction

"'How shall I a habit break?'
As you did that habit make.
As you gathered, you must lose;
As you yielded, now refuse.
Thread by thread the strands we twist
Till they bind us neck and wrist.
Thread by thread the patient hand
Must untwine ere free we stand."

-John Boyle O'Reilly

The journey to the head of the class is a commitment to excellence. The summit is a wonderful place to be!

From that great vantage point at the top, we see both the opportunities we should seize and the pitfalls to avoid. We are also able to reflect and ponder our next moves. This is why smart competitors love holding the high ground in struggles. It is the most strategic and advantageous position one can have and it is what makes winners!

In academia, striving to be at the top is a rewarding adventure. First and foremost, ignorance is a dysfunctional and destructive force. It debilitates minds and it must be fought. Smart students who value education are at the vanguard of this struggle and they are heroes. They embrace knowledge and promote its value. The collective smarts of these students at the head of the class make a better world possible for all of us.

11

Students have choices. The option to identify and climb the steps leading to the top, where the achievers of excellence reside, is one way. The opposite is also true. They can opt to practice ineffective learning habits and travel the long, winding road down into the abyss of certain failure.

For an educator, there is no greater joy than to discover a rich and engaging spirit in a student who shines brightly with imagination, creativity and a respect for the ground rules which yield the best outcomes in the teaching / learning milieu. To stand in the presence of a student experiencing a "breakthrough" moment, unraveling some mystery which previously frustrated learning, is pure delight!

Students at the head of the class have such moments. They have learned discipline and self-control and embrace every learning opportunity. They soar with the great expectation that they are – and will continue to be – part of the solutions rather than the problems of our world.

Successful students can be found in rural and city classrooms; they're male and female, from every socioeconomic background, heritage group and region in the country. What makes them stand out is that they are passionate about life and deliberate in their quest to learn and experience. They are also unwavering in their desire not to squander time and talent.

They make friends with authors by reading and studying writings with care. They search for meaning. They wrestle with ideas and seek clarification from others similarly looking for theories and paradigms to apply to solve the problems of the day. As they read and listen to lectures, they take notes and later take time to rewrite them to make them even clearer.

These students refuse to "think with their genitals." Aware of the power of uncontrolled hormones, they develop spiritual values through which they master the art of sitting on their urges. By exercising, doing physical work and participating in sports – all activities which channel and transform strong sensual energies into productive, character building virtues – these students discover the strength of a balanced life.

They make progress in their ascent to the top as educated and moral human beings. Students at the head of their class have an informed mindset which is clear about a great truth: "If you go all the way, you won't get very far."

Are there any rules to getting to the top? Successful students will tell you that there are some definite "A"s and "B"s to be earned to get to the summit where the best and brightest students reside.

These "A"s and "B"s are instructive to examine.

The first "A" is for achievement. Every positive study habit which steers you away from the pitfalls of distractions is a step up to success. Another "A" stands for aspiration. To desire above all else to be a significant force for good and be willing to go beyond the minimum by reading constantly to add value to tasks assigned by teachers is a sure way to reach one's goals.

Being assertive is the third "A." Asking for help or seeking additional clarification of concepts in need of explanation, while offering to help others in areas mastered, is key to further climbing the steps to success. Alliances with others on the long climb to the top are essential. In our diverse society, collaboration is a must. The "A" for alliances is a proud reminder that males and females, as well as traditional white males and persons from nontraditional backgrounds, need to become extensions of each other's best selves. Quality teams of people must sustain true alliances of dignity and respect. These partnerships propel everyone forward in their journey.

A "B," reflecting an above average step to the head of the class, is the one which stands for a balanced student life. A student who reads for study tasks, reflects on spiritual values, and honors loved ones through their hard work and continued advancement to the top is balanced. This balanced approach is also strengthened by a strong body, fit and made healthy through empowering recreational activities.

Another "B" stands for boldness. Against great odds, students at the head of the class face a new century in need of strategies to remove barriers and make our society safer for differences. The promise of a more prosperous future will be attained by the creative passion and boldness of those students stepping up to the head of their class.

These examples of "A"s and "B"s indicate that letter grades on report cards are not the only things that are important. The climb to the top is not solely determined by some abstract definition of a high grade point average that's largely measured by mental exercises and testing instruments.

There are students who may not get perfect grades, but should nevertheless be recognized for making excellent progress. These are the students who elevate themselves from nonacademically proficient family backgrounds. The journey before them is harder because they need to master middle class ways of knowing at the same time that they compete with others who already know how to decode learning because they are products of the middle class. These students who value education and who strive hard to learn under difficult circumstances are to be counted at the head of the class, too.

On the other hand, students who get perfect grades yet lack a balanced life – those who are not willing to lend a hand to peers in need and believe that they are superior by virtue of the accidents of class privilege and middle class nurturing – will not remain at the head of the class, for they will have ignored the "A"s and "B"s of character formation.

The way to the head of the class can be compromised by making U-turns leading downward. Stagnation is also possible. Not getting rid of dysfunctional, ineffective habits threatens progress. The steps leading up are weakened and can eventually crumble under the weight of neglect or indifference by uncaring students.

The 10 habits of dysfunctional, ineffective students must be recognized and eliminated. No student can make progress when he or she is moving in a downward direction. No one can. What follows is an in-depth discussion of these bad learning habits which block students' academic advancement.

If you are prepared to climb to the head of the class, this book is for you. Welcome! Let the following chapters be your guide.

Each chapter is framed by quotations. At the beginning are insights from major works which address educational issues. These will hopefully stir your imagination and help you focus on the topics to be discussed. The "Lasting Thoughts" at the end of each chapter are short nuggets of wisdom and witty sayings which will inspire you to continue your journey to excellence.

"You Be the Judge" is a quick exercise to help assess if you are engaged in a particular negative habit and how seriously it is impacting your progress. That is followed by the chapter itself. You are urged to read the chapter even if you believe, as a result of the "You Be the Judge" exercise, that you are doing well.

After each chapter, there is an opportunity for you to make a personal commitment to target the behaviors which stand in your way. You can also identify three partners who will join you and hold you accountable to your commitment. A bibliography is provided for those interested in further reading on educational issues and reform.

The purpose of this book is to cheer students at the top, encourage those moving up, and provide skills for others at the bottom to start the climb towards excellence. We are all cautioned to recognize and avoid habits which reverse progress and drag often unsuspecting students into the quicksand of failure.

The path from mediocrity to academic achievement must be followed, but it is not often clearly marked. This work fills that void by providing a step by step skill building map to get you there. Students at every grade level will find the lessons applicable.

Step 1

Stop Procrasti-Cramming

Lessons from the Literature

"Do not wait several days or a week to review your notes. When writing your notes very quickly, there may be some words that are actually scribbled. If a week passes before you attempt to read your notes, you may not be able to understand some of your own scribble."

-Harry G. Turner, You Can Do It! A Guide for the Adult Learner

"Remember not to be lazy. Do your homework. Pay attention to detail. Take care and pride in your work. Take the initiative in creating your own opportunity and do not wait around for other people to discover you or do you a favor. Do not assume a door is closed; push on it. Do not assume if it was closed yesterday that it is closed today. And do not ever stop learning and improving your mind, because if you do, you and America are going to be left behind."

-Marian Wright Edelman in Carrie Boyko and Kimberly Colen (Ed.), Hold Fast Your Dreams

You Be the Judge

Place an X in the box which best describes your own situation for each of the following 10 statements.

Seldom True	Often True	Most Often True	
❑	❑	❑	1. I hardly sleep the night before a test because I am frantically studying.
❑	❑	❑	2. I miss a class or call in sick to work to buy some study time.
❑	❑	❑	3. I tend to put off readings or writing papers until close to the day they are due.
❑	❑	❑	4. I tend to scout for the "better" students in class to copy their work or notes.
❑	❑	❑	5. I don't study with my friends because they do not take studying seriously.
❑	❑	❑	6. If I know there is an assignment due on a certain day, I wait until the night before to complete it.
❑	❑	❑	7. When the teacher postpones a test, I jump for joy knowing I was not really prepared.
❑	❑	❑	8. I tend to study what I feel to be the least important subjects the least amount of time.

❏   ❏   ❏   9. I work better under pressure, so it is good for me to cram.

❏   ❏   ❏   10. I blame the teacher for giving me a bad grade when I know I did not put in the time and effort to study that I should have.

Subscores:

Column 1 subscore x 1 = _____

Column 2 subscore x 2 = _____

Column 3 subscore x 3 = _____

Add all three subscores to get your total score.

Total Score: _____

If you scored:

10-15   Your perseverance is paying off. Continue your climb to the head of the class.

16-20   Caution! You are clearly slipping. Danger signs are showing. You need to take deliberate steps to change direction.

21-25   Stop procrasti-cramming! You are falling. Turn around quickly and start your climb back up.

26-30   You have crashed! Seek help immediately. While you may have hit the bottom, there is nowhere to go but up. This chapter is most definitely for you. Make a personal commitment now.

The Habit:
Procrasti-Cramming

"One of these days is none of these days."
-Henry G. Bohn

Procrastination and cramming – the two go together.
They are inseparable!

These evil twins of academic mediocrity are at the top of
the most wanted list of dangerous habits which kill
students' chances for success in the pursuit of academic
excellence.

When you welcome the first twin into your life, the
second inevitably follows. One twin holds you in check,
while the other saps creative energy from the intellect.
Putting things off till later leads to the abandoning of
fresh opportunities in the future. If you procrastinate,
you ultimately cram. These habits are combined in the
concept of "Procrasti-Cramming."

First, let's look closely at procrastination. Procrastination
is the act of putting off for tomorrow something which
should be done today. The student who does not do
assigned readings and who refuses to wrestle with
abstract formulas, concepts and ideas is not going to be
prepared to enter a class discussion.

Mastery of concepts develops in stages over time. When you put in the effort to understand and complete an assignment, you build a foundation of knowledge which comes in handy when you face your next work. Each assignment builds on previous knowledge acquired. Procrastinating sabotages those steps. Your proficiency of subject matter is derailed.

When you are not on track, you cannot travel with your non-procrastinating peers toward academic excellence. Procrastinators in fact head in the opposite direction toward academic mediocrity. The classroom experience drags. The body slumps. The mind wanders, daydreams, fantasizes or becomes cluttered. At this point, you have put yourself at risk. You are now a prime candidate for class clown, disciplinary problem student or a member of the Losers Club – a club you don't have to join if you accomplish tasks on time. Remember, if you cannot be good at being good, you probably will be good at being bad. All of us have to be good at something!

Procrastinators are hard to identify. Students who procrastinate often look and behave like those who do their work on time. Teachers find out whether procrastination has had a negative impact on you when they give a test to measure mastery of a subject matter. Test results have a way of highlighting excellence and smoking out mediocrity. Until a series of test results reflect a pattern of outcomes, it is difficult for a teacher to know if bad study habits have put a stranglehold on a student.

Procrastinating students who want to get top grades in tests find they must cram. Cramming is the medicine which makes the procrastinator feel good about being bad. That is the perception of those embracing the evil twins of Procrasti-Cramming.

Now let's take a close look at cramming. To cram is to participate in a fraud. The goal of cramming is to demonstrate instant mastery of bodies of knowledge through test results. To cram means to force thousands of bits and pieces of disconnected information into the brain through rote memorization. The game plan is to fool the teacher into believing that mastery of subject matter has been achieved through a passing test score.

After the test, the stored information is discarded as easily as a chewed up piece of gum. The information is forgotten. If a student successfully passes a test through this act of fraud, he or she is certified to be competent in a body of knowledge. This is, of course, a lie.

Author Stephen R. Covey in his work, *Principle-Centered Leadership*, notes that in nature certain laws cannot be violated without resulting in negative consequences. Without planting in the spring, a fall harvest is impossible. A farmer cannot plow, plant and water seeds 24 hours a day, two weeks before harvest time, and expect a full, rich harvest. The laws of nature simply do not operate that way.

Similarly, certain study principles have to be applied in the quest to harvest academic excellence. Attempting to shortcut the tried and true process will yield failure.

Imagine a lazy farmer who does not plant in the spring and resorts instead to buying plastic vegetables and laying them on the ground in neat rows. The imitation crops look like the real thing. Seen from a distance, the fields of produce look ripe and promising to potential buyers. But you know that the artificial, plastic substitutes are ultimately going to be revealed as a great fraud.

In the demanding marketplace of ideas, we too need serious students who will take the time to "plant in the spring," explore ideas in advance and nurture them through daily care and study so that they can yield a rich harvest. Putting off until the morrow what needs to be done today is as deadly for the student as it is for any farmer.

In the case where cramming might, in fact, cause a student to get good test results, the fraud can be deadly in its impact. The faked knowledge spells danger to professional growth and practice later on in adult life. It is mediocrity masked as deceptive excellence.

Avoid the twins of twisted logic: Procrasti-Cramming!

My Personal Commitment

I, _____ , have identified three
practices describing my habit of Procrasti-Cramming which
keep me from climbing to the head of the class.

1) _____

2) _____

3) _____

I will stop these behaviors in the following ways:

1) _____

2) _____

3) _____

I will invite the following three people to be my accountability
partners to help me climb to the head of the class.

1) _____ X. _____

2) _____ X. _____

3) _____ X. _____

Ask your accountability partners to sign their names.

X. _____ _____
      Your Signature   Date

Then...

...apply the ABCs of personal accountability by:

A   **Adjusting your behavior**

B   **Building on your progress**

C   **Continuing your collaboration**

Lasting Thoughts

"Procrastination is like a credit card: it's a lot of fun until you get the bill."

-Christopher Parker

"Putting off an easy thing makes it hard, and putting off a hard one makes it impossible."

-George H. Lonmer

"Procrastination is the art of keeping up with yesterday."

-Don Marquis

"No matter how big or soft or warm your bed is, you still have to get out of it."

-Grace Slick

"Failing to plan is planning to fail."

-Effie Jones

"Millions long for immortality who don't know what to do on a rainy afternoon."

-Susan Ertz

"Every one of you knows someone who did better than you at something in college because they approached it with slow, steady, dignified attack, rather than going for the screaming, end-of-semester, bluebook miracle."

-Cathy Guisewite

Step

2

Stop Reckless Reading

Lessons from the Literature

"I have seen many students who understand what they read but, due to an inability to figure out the meaning of new vocabulary words, answer questions about the story incorrectly... Missing the meaning of one or two key words in a story can make it appear that the child has poor comprehension, when in fact it is only a lack of vocabulary skills."

-Ricki Linksman, Solving Your Child's Reading Problems

"Reading is like looking through several windows which open to an infinite landscape. I abandon myself to the pleasure of the journey. How could I know about other people, how could I know about the history of the world, how could my mind expand and grow if I could not read? I began to read when I was very small; I learned to read and write practically when I was a baby. For me, life without reading would be like being in prison, it would be as if my spirit were in a straitjacket; life would be a very dark and narrow place."

-Isabel Allende in Nadine Rosenthal (Ed.), Speaking of Reading

You Be the Judge

Place an X in the box which best describes your own situation for each of the following 10 statements.

Seldom True	Often True	Most Often True	
❑	❑	❑	1. I become so conscious about finishing the assignment that I find myself not concentrating on what I am reading.
❑	❑	❑	2. Instead of reading the book, I watch the movie or buy the study guide.
❑	❑	❑	3. I don't stop to look up words when I read because it takes up too much time and I have other assignments I have to do as well.
❑	❑	❑	4. If I read a paragraph, even if there are words I don't understand, I still get the full meaning of the context.
❑	❑	❑	5. I tend to look up only the definitions that I know I need to know for a test.
❑	❑	❑	6. When I don't know a word, I just ask the teacher the next day.
❑	❑	❑	7. I mark or highlight a word, planning to look it up later, but end up not doing so.
❑	❑	❑	8. When I look up words in the glossary and they are not there, I don't feel I need to know them.

❑   ❑   ❑   9. I don't own a dictionary or usually
                    don't have one near me when I study.

❑   ❑   ❑   10. I do look up words I don't
                    understand but then find there are
                    words in the definition that I also
                    don't understand and just give up.

Subscores:

Column 1 subscore x 1 = _____ | Add all three
Column 2 subscore x 2 = _____ | subscores to get
Column 3 subscore x 3 = _____ | your total score.

Total Score: _____

If you scored:

10-15   Your perseverance is paying off. Continue your climb
to the head of the class.

16-20   Caution! You are clearly slipping. Danger signs are
showing. You need to take deliberate steps to change
direction.

21-25   Stop reading recklessly! You are falling. Turn around
quickly and start your climb back up.

26-30   You have crashed! Seek help immediately. While you
may have hit the bottom, there is nowhere to go but up. This
chapter is most definitely for you. Make a personal
commitment now.

The Habit:
Reckless Reading

> *"A continuous conversion…*
> *The real question is what changes will be made in you*
> *as a result of really reading a book."*
>
> -Leon Stein

Reckless reading is pretty much like reckless driving –
you continue at your own peril.

You engage in reckless reading when you don't bother to
stop to check the definition of unfamiliar words.
Continuing on prevents you from understanding the
totality of what you're reading. An undefined word in a
sentence is like a stop sign on a road. When you don't
stop at a stop sign, you increase the possibility of putting
yourself in harm's way, injuring others, wrecking your
vehicle, losing your licence or getting arrested.

Each word not understood calls for a stop sign. It is not
safe to move on until all is clear. During this pause, the
dictionary becomes essential. Using the dictionary, a
responsible reader will clear a blind spot, understand the
meaning of a new word, and make it safe to move on.

You are not the only one who can ignore a stop sign. You
must be wary of any teacher who refuses to stop. That
teacher can be so focused on finishing a portion of a

textbook that he or she instructs students to continue reading even when someone raises a hand to indicate that a word or concept is not understood.

Discerning teachers note when students misunderstand or mispronounce certain words. Yet, some teachers may just tell students to keep on reading since, they say, the meaning of the paragraph will make sense after you read the whole thing. Nonsense!

Words not understood must be properly defined. Class readings ought to come to a complete halt when a hand is raised asking for assistance. Chances are, if you are brave enough to call attention to not knowing a word or concept, you probably represent classmates in a similar situation. Such an act of courage needs to be affirmed by a caring adult.

In the absence of such a caring adult, take ownership of your need to understand the whole reading and how it connects to your journey to the head of the class. Request help from peers when you need it. Tap your parents for help. Find a proper time to challenge your teacher to guide you and your classmates in achieving excellence through reading. Chances are, one or more of these strategies will work. But if not, you must still step up to the responsibility on your own.

Another serious example of reckless reading is continuing to read even after you encounter unfamiliar concepts which you need to understand to appreciate how interrelated elements form abstract ideas. A concept not understood is a red light. Not stopping for red lights when driving will most likely cause death and destruction. The analogy holds. The message is the same. If you read without stopping to understand ideas, your ability to achieve academically will suffer.

Students must read as they should drive – conscientiously and carefully. Purchasing a summary of an assigned book as your sole study tool, watching a movie based on a given work, or simply depending on a peer or an adult's interpretation of a book are bad habits of reckless reading. A summary of a great work or a critical interpretation of a book can add value to your reading, but you must not substitute them for your own reading of the book.

To adopt someone else's views on a book generates mediocre thinking and sabotages the possibility of original thought. People experience what they read or hear in unique ways. Each individual participates in the author's story and connects the chapters to his or her own personal life, experiences and emotions.

The lazy reader will never know the value in a story, its interpretation of research or creative perspective. Imagine allowing someone else's trip to substitute for a real journey in which the reader and author meet and interact. Settling for a summary of a great book instead of enjoying the challenge of reading the author's original work can be likened to the distasteful act of savoring chewed and digested food that someone regurgitated on a platter. Disgusting!

Ultimately, reading enables you to access the world views, perspectives, dreams and interpretations of authors. Good reading must be followed by discussion with other careful readers. Together, you need to explore and apply the meaning of the author's insights to your own personal journeys. Critical thinking is enhanced by discussing and analyzing an author's work. That is why collaborative reading is an invaluable step to the head of the class.

Students who have not been nurtured in a middle class reading environment are especially challenged to read...read... read! Summer breaks must be viewed as grand opportunities for trips to the library. Experts estimate that every four books read will equal one correct answer on a verbal achievement examination. You must succeed in a middle class place called school. Our complex world, with its demanding professions and workplaces, requires constant, careful thinkers who continue to develop and improve their chances for greater success through reading.

In conclusion, I urge you to read thoroughly with care. Be conscious of your responsibility to become an autonomous learner by embracing a dictionary and taking the time to stop when you have to. This way you will be traveling on the right path on your lifelong journey of learning.

My Personal Commitment

I, _____ _____ , have identified three
practices describing my habit of Reckless Reading which keep
me from climbing to the head of the class.

1) _____ _____

2) ___ _____ _____ _____

3) _____ _____

I will stop these behaviors in the following ways:

1) _ ____ _____

2) _____ _____

3) _ _____ ___

I will invite the following three people to be my accountability
partners to help me climb to the head of the class.

1) _____ X. _ _____

2) _____ X. _____

3) _____ X. _____

Ask your accountability partners to sign their names.

X. _____ ___ _____
    Your Signature   Date

Then...

...apply the ABCs of personal accountability by:

A   **Adjusting your behavior**

B   **Building on your progress**

C   **Continuing your collaboration**

Lasting Thoughts

"Reading is to the mind what exercise is to the body."

-Joseph Addison

"Don't agonize. Organize."

-Florynce Kennedy

"Reading is... coming to know in personal terms what is in the mind of the writer."

-Harold Taylor

Step 3

Stop Fishing for Answers

Lessons from the Literature

"Today millions of English-speaking American kids enter high school unable to interpret the simplest directions, graduating without knowing how to fill out an elementary job application. They stumble through true and false tests, copy from the kid across the aisle, or play a guessing game that might give them a passing mark. Sometimes they use signals, one finger for true, two for false. Multiple-choice questions have a code: The number of fingers indicates whether the answer is A, B, C, D. I knew those tricks. I used all of them and even more."
-John Corcoran, The Teacher Who Couldn't Read

"If you answer all questions on a multiple-choice test, you are bound to get some right even if they are written in Chinese. In fact, I recently checked the standardized first-grade reading test used in our school system and, I believe, nationally and was surprised to find that thirty-two of the total of one hundred seventy-two items required a 'yes' or 'no' response. That's approximately one-fifth of the test. Now it doesn't take an expert to know that even a nonreader has a fifty-fifty chance of getting such an item right. For the whole test, the chances of guessing right are about one out of three. I don't know what the odds are at Las Vegas, but I doubt if they are much better.'
-Jack Greenstein, What the Children Taught Me

You Be the Judge

Place an X in the box which best describes your own situation for each of the following 10 statements.

Seldom True	Often True	Most Often True	
❏	❏	❏	1. I usually don't read what I am assigned because I do not have time.
❏	❏	❏	2. My teachers make up the exams based directly on the questions on study sheets so I do not have to do the readings.
❏	❏	❏	3. The teacher sometimes does not ask us to read the chapters but only to answer the questions at the end.
❏	❏	❏	4. I tend to let my friends copy my work so I have to finish quickly.
❏	❏	❏	5. My teacher explains all of the answers in class so there is no need to do the readings.
❏	❏	❏	6. I only read the chapters that will be on the exam.
❏	❏	❏	7. I do the assignment when it is due and then read the chapter just before the test.

❑ ❑ ❑ 8. The questions on the assignment highlight the main points of the chapter so I just read the paragraphs where I find the answers.

❑ ❑ ❑ 9. I get credit just for handing in the assignment. It doesn't matter if the answers are correct.

❑ ❑ ❑ 10. Sometimes the chapters are too long and boring, so I just answer the questions and move on.

Subscores:

Column 1 subscore x 1 = _____

Column 2 subscore x 2 = _____

Column 3 subscore x 3 = _____

> Add all three subscores to get your total score.

Total Score: _____

If you scored:

10-15   Your perseverance is paying off. Continue your climb to the head of the class.

16-20   Caution! You are clearly slipping. Danger signs are showing. You need to take deliberate steps to change direction.

21-25   Stop fishing for answers! You are falling. Turn around quickly and start your climb back up.

26-30   You have crashed! Seek help immediately. While you may have hit the bottom, there is nowhere to go but up. This chapter is most definitely for you. Make a personal commitment now.

The Habit:
Fishing for Answers

"Laziness may appear attractive,
but work gives satisfaction."

-Anne Frank

It's an old trick. It's easy to do. A lot of students get away
with it. Best of all, it works. Well, sort of...

It is called "fishing for answers."

You know how it goes: A teacher assigns an essay or a
section of a book to be read. To test compliance, teachers
ask students to identify some facts from the reading by
filling in the blanks on a worksheet. Usually this takes
the form of "complete the sentence" exercises. Specific
dates, names of people connected to quotations, events
and/or concepts which are associated with a definition
are filled in by students. The theory is students can only
identify these facts if they have read and studied the
assignment.

Wrong.

In fact, what often happens is some students become
expert at scanning the readings to pick out pieces of
information likely to fit into the blanks. Students who
practice this habit simply fish for the right answers. They

47

scan the sea of words in search of the prize catch that will fit neatly into the blanks. The assigned readings are not studied. The lessons are not learned. Beware, if you are guilty, you will drown in a sea of mediocrity.

There is a second "fishing" strategy. The student simply copies the correct information from someone else. That friend or classmate may in fact have copied it from a third person. In some cases, students copy answers from papers circulated by siblings or acquaintances who previously attended the same classes. What we end up with is a series of correct answers handed in on time to a teacher who may be clueless about what is going on or "care less" about the full impact of promoting a lazy way of teaching.

This practice of fishing for answers gives the illusion of providing many benefits. The best one is you get excellent grades – and this is a real big attraction. As a skilled scanner, you can also feel good when you share answers with people who then become indebted to you. Improved test results bode well for your teacher, too. Plus, your parents are happy to receive good evaluations on your schoolwork.

The time saved by fishing for answers in the book or by copying from someone else can also give you more time for play and hanging out with friends. It even saves the teacher from the laborious task of grading essays and giving specific feedback to each student. All in all, it does seem that everyone wins on this one!

When people are given choices to get from point A to point B, many apparently seek the least painful route. Confronted with the challenge of reading a whole chapter in a history text and showing evidence of having done so, it makes sense to the fishing community of students to go after the evidence directly, rather than take the more time-consuming approach of reading the entire assignment thoroughly.

But does it really work? Of course not.

The fishing metaphor is instructive in helping us to understand why this habit is very ineffective. Fishing for answers as a way of demonstrating academic competency is like announcing to friends and family that you're going fishing when, in fact, you go and play video games. Afterwards, you visit the supermarket, buy fish and return home claiming the trip was successful, showing off your big, fat, store-bought trout as evidence.

Catching fish, however, and understanding schoolwork are fundamentally different. While buying fish in the supermarket still contributes to the family meal, the consequences for the student fishing for answers has dramatically different negative results.

When you fish for answers, you shortchange yourself because you are not helping yourself acquire the ability to read and do assignments critically. The information required is not stored in the brain because you did not really study the essay or book. This leads to an inability to connect facts and apply the meaning of your learning to the challenges you are facing in life. In the end, you will sink.

Further, the mind grows lazy and the grades, diplomas and degrees are earned fraudulently. A student practicing this habit cheats everyone. Incompetent teachers are in part to blame.

How do we counteract this? A hardworking teacher can set up study circles to review assigned readings. Exciting, interactive discussions among students can follow. Definitions, dates, facts, names and events can be put into perspective. These and other strategies used by creative teachers can replace assignments that leave students to their own devices. Study strategies that render habits like "fishing for answers" useless serve as life preservers to students who would otherwise drown.

However, even in the absence of effective teaching strategies, you must resist fishing for answers as the key to supercharging your grades. As a young and honest spirit in search of true education, you must turn your back on superficiality. Reject illusions. Avoid guesswork. Invest in yourself. The wise student will respect a process which may take greater effort but will yield both correct answers and an in-depth understanding of what is assigned to be read.

Too many students fish for answers and get away with scoring well in homework and examinations. While this habit may reap quick and easy results, the long-term buildup of shortcuts weakens one's integrity considerably. The deception can be tragic. This ineffective habit is the bait that hooks you into becoming the sorriest fish in the sea of mediocrity.

Multiple choice, true or false, fill in the blanks – all these belong to a family of worksheets which can be manipulated by guesswork. Students can guess and pass. But they will not learn how to apply knowledge, formulas and theories, communicate more effectively, think more clearly and become universalized. If you decide to turn your back on the practice of fishing for answers, you must also avoid answering test questions or completing assignments simply through guesswork. Step up to the challenge of self-discipline and self-control as you make continuous progress to the head of the class.

My Personal Commitment

I, _____ , have identified three
practices describing my habit of Fishing for Answers which
keep me from climbing to the head of the class.

1) _____

2) _____

3) _____

I will stop these behaviors in the following ways:

1) _____

2) _____

3) _____

I will invite the following three people to be my accountability
partners to help me climb to the head of the class.

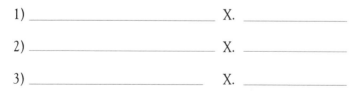

1) _____ X. _____

2) _____ X. _____

3) _____ X. _____

Ask your accountability partners to sign their names.

X. _____ _____

      Your Signature   Date

Then...

...apply the ABCs of personal accountability by:

A   **Adjusting your behavior**

B   **Building on your progress**

C   **Continuing your collaboration**

Lasting Thoughts

"There is a country in Europe where multiple-choice tests are illegal."

-Sigfried Hulzer

"I find that the harder I work, the more luck I seem to have."

-Thomas Jefferson

Step 4

Stop Post-Lecture Reading

Lessons from the Literature

"Daddy used to ask us whether the teacher gave us any homework and if we said no, he said, well, assign yourself some. Do not wait around for somebody else to direct you to do what you are able to figure out and do for yourself. Do not do just as little as you can do to get by."
-*Marian Wright Edelman in Carrie Boyko and Kimberly Colen (Ed.)*, Hold Fast Your Dreams

"Literature is my Utopia. Here I am not disenfranchised. No barrier of the senses shuts me out from the sweet, gracious discourse of my book friends. They talk to me without embarrassment or awkwardness."
-*Helen Keller in Carolyn Warner (Ed.)*, Treasury of Women's Quotations

You Be the Judge

Seldom True	Often True	Most Often True	
❑	❑	❑	1. I tend to wait until after class to do the readings because then I know exactly what I have to read.
❑	❑	❑	2. Some of my teachers never give quizzes, so I do not read until I have the time.
❑	❑	❑	3. Some of my teachers do not call on me to answer questions so I don't bother to prepare.
❑	❑	❑	4. Participation does not count towards my grade, so I don't usually read before class.
❑	❑	❑	5. I sometimes have so much homework the night before class that I just postpone any reading so I can finish other assignments.
❑	❑	❑	6. I never read anything until just before the exam so that the information is fresh in my mind.
❑	❑	❑	7. Sometimes I don't go to class because I am not prepared that day.

❑	❑	❑	8. Since we read and look over the chapters in class, I would waste time if I were to read it twice.
❑	❑	❑	9. I can psyche out the teacher and can tell what will be on the test. I only read for that.
❑	❑	❑	10. My teachers tend to assign readings which are never covered on any test, so it would be a waste of time to read the material.

Subscores:

Column 1 subscore x 1 = _____
Column 2 subscore x 2 = _____
Column 3 subscore x 3 = _____

> Add all three subscores to get your total score.

Total Score: _____

If you scored:

10-15   Your perseverance is paying off. Continue your climb to the head of the class.

16-20   Caution! You are clearly slipping. Danger signs are showing. You need to take deliberate steps to change direction.

21-25   Stop post-lecture reading! You are falling. Turn around quickly and start your climb back up.

26-30   You have crashed! Seek help immediately. While you may have hit the bottom, there is nowhere to go but up. This chapter is most definitely for you. Make a personal commitment now.

The Habit:
Post-Lecture Reading

> *"It's better to be prepared for an opportunity
> and not have one than to have an opportunity
> and not be prepared."*
>
> Whitney Young

A class lecture is usually based on assigned readings.

When a student does not do the readings before a
scheduled class discussion, he or she is taking a
calculated risk that the teacher will not give a quiz on
the material and that the readings can be done before
any major exam. Often, the student is also assuming that
he or she will not really have to do all of the readings
since listening to the lecture will most likely highlight
the information the teacher will select to put in an
examination.

What drives this calculated risk is often the student's
desire to manage time. Time spent reading is time taken
away from other priorities. From the student's point of
view, post-lecture reading is the logical choice given
competing activities in a short time frame.

There are different strategies to fake knowledge about
what readings might contain, just in case a surprise quiz
is announced or the student is called on in class. Quick

debriefing conversations with the class whiz on a summary of the contents may be complemented by scanning the chapter in question. Reading the headings and the closing paragraph in the assigned chapter is another typical shortcut. Cheating by glancing at another student's paper during a pop quiz, or simply guessing at true or false or even multiple choice questions are also easy outs for the unprepared. To their surprise and delight, students find these strategies work and they are able to get by.

Savvy students who tend to do post-lecture reading bank on their ability to psyche out the teacher. Students often correctly predict their teacher's behavior. For example, after a major test has been given, it is expected that the teacher will not "spoil" the next class by giving a quiz. The assumption that teachers are prepared to give students a breather after a period of rigorous preparation for a test leads some students to abandon reading assignments right afterwards. In college settings, some students do not even attend the class period following an examination.

Post-lecture reading is prompted by a disposition which says, "Don't read. Wait until it is absolutely necessary." By that, students tend to mean that until some measurable accounting mechanism is put in place by the system, readings do not have to be done. "Wait until you have to study for a test, then do the readings." Or "Wait until you are forced to read, then read the minimum requirement."

In deciding what students need to master for an examination, teachers will sometimes announce which sections will or will not be covered. This tends to happen when teachers depend on exams prepared by book publishers. Teachers decide on a certain number of questions and assign only those sections in a text covered in the exams. This, of course, perpetuates the notion that one only has to read the minimum to pass an exam. If there is evidence that the information in the readings is not going to be tested, it is likely that students will ignore those sections completely.

Just what is so bad about post-lecture reading? Why does it matter? The question really boils down to what your educational objective is – to pass an exam or to learn concepts and examine points of view?

Post-lecture readers are more interested in obtaining a certificate to be hung on a wall than in achieving the proficiency which can be applied to solving problems and improving our quality of life. When you read to satisfy the demands of an outside authority, you have an erroneous sense of the function and impact of reading on human understanding.

Reading strengthens the power of the brain to be analytical. Reading adds value and heightens the potential for meaning-making in the pursuit of understanding. Reading sharpens a person's point of view by providing counter-points derived from diverse opinions.

You reap the benefits of an informed forum when you have the dynamic interplay between the instructor's views, the ideas and opinions of the authors in the assigned readings and the insights of all the members of the class who participate actively in discussion. The resulting forum makes full use of the range of perspectives present.

Students who do not do the assigned readings before the class discussion retard their growth and that of others. They show up at the forum with a voluntary, self-inflicted disability. They limit their contribution by not coming as prepared members of the team. They choose to remain ignorant about a point of view, often thinking that no one is likely to know or, perhaps, even care. They fail to understand that the pursuit of education must find its purpose within the self not from some outside force.

Teachers can only guide willing learners. To read something only to pass a test makes a mockery of education. To read and study before a class lecture is to prepare for full citizenship in the community of learners. This process will create opportunities for the exchange of ideas. The examination or test is merely an instrument to enhance concentration and help commit to memory some important concepts which can be used to think abstractly.

Reading to learn how to learn is the best reading of all. Self-directed reading is most fruitful. Information acquired through reading increases your competency to carry your fair share of ideas, which are then filtered through personal perspectives, shared with others and celebrated in a common commitment not only to learn from others but also to teach.

The passport to effective participation in the classroom is pre-lecture reading. Without preparation, there is no entry into the community of learners. You will be banned from climbing the ladder to success.

My Personal Commitment

I,_____ , have identified three practices describing my habit of Post-lecture Reading which keep me from climbing to the head of the class.

1) _____

2) _____

3) _____

I will stop these behaviors in the following ways:

1) _____

2) _____

3) _____

I will invite the following three people to be my accountability partners to help me climb to the head of the class.

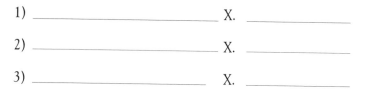

1) _____ X. _____

2) _____ X. _____

3) _____ X. _____

Ask your accountability partners to sign their names.

X. _____ _____
    Your Signature   Date

Then...

...apply the ABCs of personal accountability by:

A   Adjusting your behavior

B   Building on your progress

C   Continuing your collaboration

Lasting Thoughts

"Waiting is a trap. There will always be reasons to wait...
The truth is, there are only two things in life, reasons
and results, and reasons simply don't count."
-Robert Anthony

"If I couldn't read, I couldn't live."
-Thelma Green

Step 5

Stop Loafing in the Place of Study

Lessons from the Literature

"Since the Japanese attribute academic success to effort, their students work harder than their American counterparts, whose society attributes success to inborn ability. The lesson we can learn from the overly envied Japanese education system is that it's okay to have to try hard when learning doesn't come easily; the only blame comes from not trying."
-*Mary Susan Miller*, Save Our Schools

"Good listeners hear a message, are focused, assimilate the information for understanding and respond accordingly. The process of staying focused refers to the ability to identify distractions, which become barriers to effective listening, and eliminate them."
-*Harry G. Turner*, You Can Do It! A Guide for the Adult Learner

You Be the Judge

Place an X in the box which best describes your own situation for each of the following 10 statements.

Seldom True	Often True	Most Often True	
❏	❏	❏	1. I tend to study in bed.
❏	❏	❏	2. I talk on the phone or hang out with friends when I should be studying.
❏	❏	❏	3. I sometimes have the television on while I study.
❏	❏	❏	4. During study hall, my mind wanders, I doze off, and I use the time as an opportunity for rest.
❏	❏	❏	5. When at the library, I tend to sleep or look at magazines to counter boredom.
❏	❏	❏	6. I do not take many notes while in class because I am paying attention to other things or because it doesn't seem to help.
❏	❏	❏	7. My room is so disorganized and sloppy it is hard to find a clear, clean space where I can concentrate on my homework.

❏　　❏　　❏　　8. I don't study in study hall because I feel more comfortable studying at home.

❏　　❏　　❏　　9. Sometimes I do not have any school work to do in study hall so I just mess around.

❏　　❏　　❏　　10. My parents make me study at home before I can have any fun anyway so I don't study at school.

Subscores:

Column 1 subscore x 1 = _____

Column 2 subscore x 2 = _____

Column 3 subscore x 3 = _____

> Add all three subscores to get your total score.

Total Score: _____

If you scored:

10-15　　Your perseverance is paying off. Continue your climb to the head of the class.

16-20　　Caution! You are clearly slipping. Danger signs are showing. You need to take deliberate steps to change direction.

21-25　　Stop loafing in the place of study! You are falling. Turn around quickly and start your climb back up.

26-30　　You have crashed! Seek help immediately. While you may have hit the bottom, there is nowhere to go but up. This chapter is most definitely for you. Make a personal commitment now.

The Habit:
Loafing in The Place of Study

"Just go out there and do what you've got to do."
- *Martina Navratilova*

Study Hall – the scheduled period in a class day during which students in the upper grades are required to be in school but not in a subject class. During this period, students are encouraged to study.

At least in theory, study hall is an oasis, an opportunity for students to work on academic requirements at their own discretion. They are to demonstrate maturity to themselves and to their peers by exercising self-control and self-directed learning. The reality, however, is vastly different from the theory. For far too many students, the reality is best described as the highly ineffective habit of "loafing in the place of study."

What really happens during study hall? Check out this list. You will recognize it.
- Sleeping
- Fake reading
- Browsing through magazines or books with pictures
- Cutting classes
- Signaling friends across the way
- Daydreaming
- Gossiping

- A lot of posturing and seeking attention from the opposite sex
- Making paper airplanes
- Writing love notes
- Throwing spit balls
- Playing mini video games
- Cramming for an upcoming examination

"Anything but study in study hall" is the way my colleague, Shawn Surber, described it.

In some cases, parents ask their children to wait for them in the library after school. The library becomes a hangout for a new generation of "latch key kids." It seldom occurs to library staff to do much more than demand silence. Teachers don't always nurture reading habits which could benefit well from regular visits to the library. Instead, the library is viewed simply as a waiting station for bored students to just loaf around.

College students may be tempted to view the library as a quiet, soothing place of escape. The study cubicles beckon the weary to lay their heads in a repose mode instead of a study mode. Opportunities for studying in the library are squandered. When libraries are not used for study, they often become centers of cramming on the eve of exams.

There's a big irony in all of this. When students waste precious time loafing in the place of study, they end up wanting to study in a place of rest. It is not unusual for some students to try to study, cram or do some of their required reading in bed. A bed is for sleeping, not for studying. To lie in bed with a book or set of notes by one's side is to pit the desire to rest squarely against the need to be mentally alert to tackle abstract ideas. And you know what? Sleep almost always wins out.

The kitchen, dinner table, living room, bathroom and bedroom all serve specific primary functions. Our bodies are predisposed to the stimulation suggested by those primary functions. For the eyes to transmit a message to the brain that a very comfortable bed is in sight and for the head to feel embraced by a soft pillow is to program the person for rest and sleep.

Placing a book in your hand to be stared at by eyes, which have been deactivated as part of the brain's shutdown of its mental alertness program, spells disaster if you're planning to study. Why should anyone expect otherwise when the body has been given orders to quit thinking and start snoozing? The habit of taking a study challenge to bed is ineffective. It must be stopped.

What is the right recipe for studying effectively? Students need a proper space for study. A comfortable chair, notes with clear directions from the teacher, a proper rest period to predispose the mind to mental alertness all do wonders to help you read, absorb, analyze and understand your assignments. It also helps if you team up with someone who, like you, is striving to excel.

Then there is music. Some people like studying with music in the background. But I caution you, choose your music carefully.

You won't be able to focus on studying if you have soulful, love songs tugging at your emotions, stimulating sensual feelings or arousing fantasies. The same goes for rhythmic music that sets feet tapping, hips swinging or makes you want to sing! What about relaxing music? It's true, some classical music or soft instrumentals may create a mood for reflective study, but it is not for everyone. Young folks unaccustomed to classical music may find it distracting as a study prop.

For the most part, students enjoy the music of MTV and the Top 40 stations. This music has its time and place, but not in study period. Perfectly suited for fun and celebration, these sounds collide head on with the need for mental clarity when it's time to study. In the end, music may simply prove to be too much of a distraction. You must be aware of that.

The same principle applies to any stimulation of the senses which leap out of music videos, sports programs, TV sitcoms, cartoons, movies and ads. These media products have but one goal in mind – to capture your undivided attention and keep you away from the competition. The real danger is when studying becomes the competition. What you need to appreciate is that, while educational programs are often presented in boring, passive frameworks, they are a lot more important to concentrate on right now if you are to enjoy leisure and well-earned loafing moments later on.

Success at becoming a competent member of the workforce, a responsible citizen and a healthy human being is a direct result of learning to get rid of lousy habits. Every obstacle which detracts from and frustrates your journey towards educational success must be avoided. My advice to you: seize study time for study; stop loafing; start learning; be self directed.

Never take a vacation from learning. The break periods between semesters and academic years provide willing learners wonderful opportunities for continued growth. Do not waste these long breaks by taking a leave of absence from learning. Build your vocabulary skills through reading. Keep your mental muscles exercised. Make use of the dictionary. Join a reading or discussion group. If one is not established in your community, start one. Be prepared to reconnect with your learning adventure by having a strong mind, being informed and being engaged in the world of ideas.

Bear in mind that many of the students from middle class families, where reading is nurtured, never stop reading even during summer breaks. They continue to increase their vocabulary and position themselves to enter the new school year already mentally alert. The long summer breaks are not for loafing. They are a time for continual learning, especially through the joy of reading, reading and more reading.

When you take charge of your own learning and discipline yourself to stay focused on your quest for knowledge, you demonstrate that you have learned the greatest lesson of all – you have learned to learn!

My Personal Commitment

I, _____ , have identified three
practices describing my habit of Loafing in the Place of Study
which keep me from climbing to the head of the class.

1) _____

2) _____

3) _____

I will stop these behaviors in the following ways:

1) _____

2) _____

3) _____

I will invite the following three people to be my accountability
partners to help me climb to the head of the class.

1) _____ X. _____

2) _____ X. _____

3) _____ X. _____

Ask your accountability partners to sign their names.

X. _____ _____
   Your Signature   Date

Then...

...apply the ABCs of personal accountability by:

A   Adjusting your behavior

B   Building on your progress

C   Continuing your collaboration

Lasting Thoughts

"Leisure is a beautiful garment, but it will not do for constant wear."

-Anonymous

"What success I achieved in the theater is due to the fact that I have always worked just as hard where there were ten people in the house as when there were thousands. Just as hard in Springfield, Illinois as on Broadway."

-Bill "Bojangles" Robinson

"It's not so much how busy you are, but why you are busy. The bee is praised; the mosquito is swatted."

-Marie O'Conner

"Talk doesn't cook rice."

-Chinese Proverb

Step 6

Stop Going Solo

Lessons from the Literature

"The real world demands collaboration, the collective solving of problems. The clichés are familiar: Two minds are better than one. Many hands make light work. Learning to get along, to function effectively in a group, is essential. Evidence and experience also strongly suggest that an individual's personal learning is enhanced by collaborative effort. The act of sharing ideas, of having to put one's own views clearly to others, of finding defensible compromises and conclusions, is in itself educative."

-Theodore R. Sizer, Horace's School

"How far can we go together... men and women, black, brown, yellow, white, young and old? We will go as far as we can because we must go wherever it is we are going together. There is no such thing as going alone."

-Michael Ventura in Vernon E. Lattin, Rolando Hinojosa, and Gary D. Keller (Eds.), Tomás Rivera: The Man and His Work

You Be the Judge

Place an X in the box which best describes your own situation for each of the following 10 statements.

Seldom True	Often True	Most Often True	
❏	❏	❏	1. I do not have that many friends with whom I can easily study.
❏	❏	❏	2. I have read or learned something on my own which I thought had a singular meaning only to find out in a class discussion that there were actually many meanings.
❏	❏	❏	3. I do not like studying with other people because they will steal my ideas and cheat.
❏	❏	❏	4. When I study with other people they sometimes do not listen to anyone else and only want to be heard.
❏	❏	❏	5. Usually, I do not need any help.
❏	❏	❏	6. When I try to study with my friends, we end up not studying and just fool around.
❏	❏	❏	7. I feel I work faster when I study by myself.
❏	❏	❏	8. I am most comfortable studying in my own house or in my own room.

❑ ❑ ❑ 9. There have been times when I needed information I did not have and could not get because I did not know anyone in my class to contact.

❑ ❑ ❑ 10. Even when I need help, I am too embarrassed to ask anyone.

Subscores:

Column 1 subscore x 1 = _____

Column 2 subscore x 2 = _____

Column 3 subscore x 3 = _____

> Add all three subscores to get your total score.

Total Score: _____

If you scored:

10-15   Your perseverance is paying off. Continue your climb to the head of the class.

16-20   Caution! You are clearly slipping. Danger signs are showing. You need to take deliberate steps to change direction.

21-25   Stop going solo! You are falling. Turn around quickly and start your climb back up.

26-30   You have crashed! Seek help immediately. While you may have hit the bottom, there is nowhere to go but up. This chapter is most definitely for you. Make a personal commitment now.

The Habit:
Going Solo

*"If you have knowledge,
let others light their candles in it."*

- Margaret Fuller

Studying alone can be deadly.

When studying, you really want to understand and recall
the important ideas. The best way to learn and
remember is to share, compare and review lessons being
learned with others. While engaged in study, the human
mind has to separate solid ideas from weak or vague ones.
It does this best through dialogue and collaboration.

When people communicate, exchange information,
clarify abstract concepts, work out formulas and consider
competing opinions, they tend to hold on to strong ideas
made clearer through such interactions. Real learning
happens through the tension of communicating
knowledge with other complex and thinking human
beings. Going solo just doesn't cut it.

Learning takes root when others, who have your best
interest at heart, challenge your assumptions, seek
insights, give feedback, correct errors, press for
consistency, add value by sharing illustrations, and
provide alternative perspectives. It is a dynamic process
and it works!

A way to determine the breadth, depth and relevance of your ideas is to place them under the spotlight and scrutiny of a caring, critical and concerned peer or peers to get feedback on how to improve your perspectives. This process is called collaboration.

By giving permission to a study partner or partners to help, you will be challenged to provide reasons for your point of view. Team members, in turn, provide feedback and add value to what you believe to be the best explanation on a given topic. All benefit from this creative engagement. In the end, you achieve greater precision and focus.

By forming tight, respectful relationships in your course of study, you will make or strengthen friendships through the adventure of learning together. An added benefit is that teachers are more likely to respond to a group of students seeking help and clarification.

Studying solo is thinking in isolation. You squander the opportunity to sift ideas through various filters or frameworks. It is invaluable for you to receive feedback from other students traveling the same educational journey. By talking a lesson through with open-minded friends or classmates, you are enhancing your learning.

The future requires that people work in teams. Study teams prepare students for challenges in the workplace, community and family endeavors. In his wonderful and very readable book, *Teamwork*, Bob Gartner writes:

Teamwork is all around you: at home, at school, at work. Meeting with a group of friends to study for tests or organizing an event with an after-school club are examples of teamwork in school... Teamwork is an important part of your future, too. Sure, you're becoming more independent, but working well with others is one of the things that will help you make it on your own. Employers notice employees who are "team players." Working well with groups of people is a skill you will need your whole life.

Get together and compare notes on an assignment. Talk about how it should be presented to the teacher and when it is due. Plan ahead. Seek clarification from your study partners. Share your thoughts when others stand to benefit from your insights. Don't go solo. When studying in teams, agree on which part of the assignment is to be done separately before you get together again to compare and contrast each unique way of addressing the issues.

Following that, some discussion on how to apply what has been learned as a proper response to assignments must take place. Finally, talk about the best way to help each other prepare for exams or class evaluations which are sure to follow at the conclusion of the course or section of study.

Caution: Avoid showing up at a discussion group ill-prepared. Make it clear, through your own example, that study groups require all members to do their job by coming informed and eager to contribute. The worse thing is to milk the thinking of others without contributing. Study teams must not be corrupted by becoming cramming sessions for procrastinators. By doing their fair share of the work, team members will add value to other participants eager to step up to the head of the class.

Tutors learn a lot more than the person being tutored. When you explain something to someone else, it becomes clearer in your own mind. The reason why teachers tend to know a great deal more than students has to do, in part, with their constant challenge of explaining and sharing their knowledge with new generations of students.

Individual students pose new challenges by asking questions and presenting different scenarios to a teacher. That type of interaction forces discussion. Out of this energy, debate and wrestling with comparative frameworks, the mind of every person engaged in the dialogue is strengthened. Definitions are sharpened. And the capacity for greater abstract thinking mushrooms into greater heights of academic excellence.

Welcome tutors and teachers into your life. Become a person who learns from and teaches others. By asking and receiving assistance from someone else, you are actually helping the other person become sharper and more familiar with the body of knowledge that you are also mastering. The best students simply become better students through collaborative exchanges with those in need of tutoring. By giving badly needed guidance to another person, you receive the blessing of strengthening your own capabilities.

Partnerships are absolutely necessary to achieve academic proficiency. They promote greater understanding of concepts and deeper learning of subject matter. The habit of going solo – talking to the air, reading silently and wrestling with ideas alone – limits the energy and electricity which come from being connected to additional sources of creative power and imagination.

Reading creative pieces of work to others for feedback is very valuable. Networking with people other than in a school study team is also effective. Tapping parents or siblings, a quick phone call to a classmate or communicating by e-mail or fax with someone not accessible for a face to face sit-down are different approaches which can help.

The idea is to get feedback, incorporate recommendations and approach subject matter from diverse points of view. Collaboration will make you wiser and more proficient as a result of the help you will receive. It will improve your grades. You will find yourself more appreciated, applauded and celebrated as a true friend by those who learn from your insights, points of view and creative genius.

Getting to the top of the class with these support networks will be easier and more efficient. It will also likely bring a lot more satisfaction than going at it alone.

Going solo? Not on your academic life.

My Personal Commitment

I, _____ , have identified three practices describing my habit of Going Solo which keep me from climbing to the head of the class.

1) _____

2) _____

3) _____

I will stop these behaviors in the following ways:

1) _____

2) _____

3) _____

I will invite the following three people to be my accountability partners to help me climb to the head of the class.

1) _____ X. _____

2) _____ X. _____

3) _____ X. _____

Ask your accountability partners to sign their names.

X. _____ _____
      Your Signature   Date

Then...

...apply the ABCs of personal accountability by:

A   **Adjusting your behavior**

B   **Building on your progress**

C   **Continuing your collaboration**

Lasting Thoughts

"Loneliness is the most terrible poverty."

-Mother Teresa

He was more than a friend,
he was family to me.
Yet, there was something about him,
that made me proud to be just me.

-Richard Guel (Age 12)

A Friend is...

"In prosperity a pleasure, a solace in adversity, in grief a comfort, in joy a merry companion, at all other times an other I."

-Adapted from John Lyly

"A true friend unbosoms freely, advises justly, assists readily, adventures boldly, takes all patiently, defends courageously, and continues a friend unchangeably."

William Penn

"We are, all of us, molded and remolded by those who touch our lives. No one can cross the paths of our destiny without leaving some mark upon it forever."

-Anonymous

Step 7

Stop Viewing Teachers as Adultists

Lessons from the Literature

"...adultism includes thinking of young people as delicate and helpless, underestimating their abilities, thinking of young people as an age category rather than individual people, being amazed if a young person has a good idea or says something very intelligent, requiring young people to sit still for long periods of time (it is the adults who are irrational in this respect) and to submit to the general indignities of school, and using youngness as a put-down (i.e., 'act your age,' 'you're acting like a kid')."
-Shelia Rose in The Caring Parent, No. 1

"Conversely, the typical street corner student has experienced a life that is characteristic of very poor families. Discipline has been inconsistent, harsh and physical. Ridicule is used; punishment is based on whether his behavior bothered his parents. He was controlled largely physically and there was limited verbal communication within the family. There was little acceptance of him as an individual. He was most often reared through authoritarian methods. His mother usually ran the house and, when his father was home, he was primarily a punitive figure."
-Herbert L. Foster, Ribbin' Jivin' & Playing the Dozens

You Be the Judge

Place an X in the box which best describes your own situation for each of the following 10 statements.

Seldom True	Often True	Most Often True	
❏	❏	❏	1. I have a tendency to talk back to teachers so they can get a taste of how it feels to be bossed around.
❏	❏	❏	2. I do not care how big or old or how many degrees a teacher has. If the teacher gives me orders to do things, I won't do them without putting up a fight.
❏	❏	❏	3. The problem with teachers is that they tend to be like pushy parents, always telling me what to do.
❏	❏	❏	4. All teachers tend to be insensitive to the needs of students.
❏	❏	❏	5. If teachers do not tell me to complete a task in a very nice way, I will ignore their direction.
❏	❏	❏	6. I cannot wait to get out of school so I can catch my breath and be far away from adults who behave as though their only purpose in life is to make young people miserable.

❑ ❑ ❑ 7. My parents are always pushing me around, telling me to do this and that, and I have to take it from them, but I will not accept the same treatment from adults in my school.

❑ ❑ ❑ 8. I tend to resist doing things in school the way the teachers want them done or at the time they want them done.

❑ ❑ ❑ 9. Too many teachers have the attitude that when it comes to doing anything, it it is their way or no way.

❑ ❑ ❑ 10. I tend to sit in the back row of the classroom, avoiding being called on by the teacher. I'm afraid of saying something wrong or putting teachers in a position to tell me what to do.

Subscores:

Column 1 subscore x 1 = _____
Column 2 subscore x 2 = _____
Column 3 subscore x 3 = _____

| Add all three subscores to get your total score. |

Total Score: _____

If you scored:

10-15   Your perseverance is paying off. Continue your climb to the head of the class.

16-20   Caution! You are clearly slipping. Danger signs are showing. You need to take deliberate steps to change direction.

21-25   Stop viewing teachers as adultists! You are falling. Turn around quickly and start your climb back up.

26-30   You have crashed! Seek help immediately. While you may have hit the bottom, there is nowhere to go but up. This chapter is most definitely for you. Make a personal commitment now.

The Habit:
Viewing Teachers as Adultists

"Whatever games are played with us,
we must play no games with ourselves."

-Ralph Waldo Emerson

Adultists exist. They are people in your life who erroneously believe that because they are older, they automatically command respect. As a result, they become pushy, demanding, inflexible and abusive. In turn, you resist following their directives. You become passive aggressive, drag your feet or absent yourself from their presence as much as possible.

If these adultists are also your parents, you tend to adopt a love-hate relationship with them. If you can't talk back for fear of being slapped or losing privileges, you mutter counter hostilities under your breath and may even do deviant things to protest your being victimized. Worse, you may also have older siblings following in your parents' dreadful footsteps, being pushy and disrespectful. If you have younger siblings, you too may behave like an adultist by pushing them around. This vicious cycle causes young people to think of elders as "enemies." If you have been shaped in that type of social environment, be on alert. You are at risk of becoming a disciplinary problem in your school life.

We grow up thinking that adults in positions of authority are bound to be like our parents. If you are shaped by loving parents, parents who discipline but do not punish and who are guided by a sense of fairness, you will likely look upon adults as worthy of admiration and trust – not as adultists.

The reverse is also true. If your parents behave like boorish adultists, they will likely poison your view and you'll grow up generally thinking that adults are uncaring, selfish and unworthy of respect.

Viewing adults as the enemy, you may feel a need to confront them and derail their plans. And since teachers are adults in positions of authority, you may very well target them with antisocial behavior because of previous experience with adultists in your life.

Let's identify the behavioral characteristics of adultists. They are likely to be pushy, demanding, overbearing older persons. Their most debilitating actions project the message that older people do not really care about the feelings of the young people around them. Adults who believe they are important by virtue of their parental status constitute the classic adultists.

See if you recognize this scene. Your father or mother comes home, walks into the TV room and, without the least concern for what you or others may be in the middle of watching, simply clicks away to whatever program suits his or her fancy. You have just been ignored. Your self-worth has just been diminished. You feel humiliated. You are burning up inside, but helpless to do anything about it. It really hurts a lot, especially when these insensitive figures also happen to be your parents. It doesn't help that you depend on them for food, shelter, clothing and much more.

Adultists give all authority figures a bad reputation when they callously interrupt your conversation with friends to send you on errands, unaware and/or unconcerned about the activity they just interrupted. If adultists believe that you are not responding fast enough, they won't think twice about being abusive to you even in front of your peers. Ouch! That really hurts.

Adultists can suffocate your inner self. They tell you what to do so often, you come to the conclusion that you don't want to do anything. You give up believing in yourself. But when you shut out teachers who are caring and true to their vocation, you close the door to the process by which you can achieve true greatness.

In many instances, adultists demand obedience on command. They loaf around, reading newspapers or magazines, watching TV and yelling out orders. "Answer the phone!" "Empty the ashtray!" "Get me a drink!" "Take out the garbage!" "Get out of my sight!" Each order is packaged in an urgent, threatening tone of voice. There is no room for objection. You must stop whatever you are doing and obey. In the adultist mind, children have no rights that adults need to respect. They really believe this atrocious behavior is justified. When they were growing up, they were probably treated in an abusive, pushy manner and now they do the same. They rationalize the demand for unquestioning obedience and respect for authority thinking that young ones under their charge are learning responsibility. The same garbage they were fed is what they now serve to the next generation. They may go as far as believing that they are building character and good work habits in their children through their harshness.

To adultists, young children were put into the world to do the bidding of older people. The pushed, punished and disrespected victims are sent to school. These students enter school prepared to reject adultist behavior. All adults are adultists, they think. At school, they act out. They are headed for trouble with teachers, peers, principals, counselors and, above all, with themselves. They are not headed to the top of the class. Check your attitude. If you resist positive adult leadership, could it be that you have been shaped by a dysfunctional adultist?

If you are a product of an adultist upbringing and want to succeed in school, stop and think about the forces which might propel you towards academic failure. You are likely to expect the worst from teachers. Especially when teachers display a no-nonsense attitude, are strict and demand accountability from all students. You may confuse directives to accomplish tasks by a positive, forceful teacher as crass disregard for your dignity, humanity and freedom. In your eyes, such teachers must be resisted. You enter school ready to defy anyone representing authority.

Acts of defiance do not have to be vicious, explosive in nature, or full of rage to have a deadly impact. Students become very sophisticated at learning how to push the right buttons aimed at getting teachers upset, without crossing the line which can earn them a quick trip to the principal's office or a suspension. It starts when a student withdraws a sense of respect or awe for an adult as an educator. That is the first step which pits student against teacher.

A disrespectful spirit encourages further acts of defiance. Many of these acts are passive in nature. Some are not. However, all of them spell disaster by making schools places of hostility and conflict. Students become indifferent to class assignments. Walking into the classroom is done with calculated lethargy. Finding a seat takes forever. Slamming books on desks is not uncommon. They have mastered the art of sitting with an "I don't care" attitude. There is no disposition to sit erect, no eagerness to learn or to become engaged in the dialogue and tasks which guide the process of learning.

Defiant students also talk when they should be listening and remain silent when invited to express their ideas. At times they write obscenities in their textbooks. They raise their hands more often to ask permission to go to the bathroom than to make a contribution and add value to the learning happening in the classroom. They also encourage other students who act like bullies or fools in the classroom. They pester or try to intimidate serious students. It is not unusual for sexual or racial harassment to become a part of the defiance. In numerous ways, these students terrorize the classroom and poison the peaceful climate for a healthy learning experience. As a result, no predictable progress to the head of the class is possible.

Troublemakers in the classroom are often so successful at creating chaos, frustrating both teaching and learning, that they cause new teachers entering the profession to abandon their ideals or desire to teach where the needs are greatest. Teachers, who are emotionally rejected by students, withdraw respect and affection in return. Once the classroom is transformed into a war zone, learning becomes the greatest casualty. When enough bad experiences frighten teachers into reacting harshly to get their turf back, don't be surprised if you wind up with an adultist, even if you didn't start out with one.

Being an anti-hero, pushing buttons to sabotage the teaching/learning agenda and intentionally displaying disrespectful body language against teachers as symbols of authority become more enjoyable than fulfilling the teacher's requirements. In the end, everybody loses. But you lose the most since you will lack the proficiency to make positive contributions in life. In becoming a problem to others, you sabotage your own growth.

This downward spiral toward self-destruction must be stopped. You must give teachers opportunities to demonstrate that they care, that they are worthy of respect. In some cases their own behavior may reflect classic adultist practices, for teachers are people too. They have strengths and weaknesses. They need to be challenged in positive ways to change. But to stereotype all teachers as abusive adults is not fair. To assume that teachers are more likely than not to behave as adultists is not fair either. The ideal is to expect that, as professionals, teachers are more inclined to help, guide and win you over through a caring, respectful and sensitive approach in educational endeavors.

If you have been a victim of adultist behavior, learn to break the cycle. The first step is to acknowledge that not all teachers are adultists. Wanting to build respectful relationships with adults in positions of authority is a necessary second step. The third step is to collaborate with caring, respectful and sensitive teachers.

Many indignities may clutter your road to learning and maturity. You may encounter adultist, racist, sexist and otherwise insensitive people along the way. But you will also find many good people seeking to provide assistance along that same journey.

When someone offers to help, gives you an assignment, clarifies a concept, guides you into a different or better way to view a challenge, you must smile. Express gratitude. Do what they require as you widen your horizons and universalize your spirit. Expect teachers to teach you and counselors to counsel. They will give you demanding class work to sharpen your insights and make you more academically aware. Don't be rude. Don't aggravate the lives of professional people seeking to discipline you towards success.

Remember, get rid of the habit of viewing all teachers as adultists. If you get rid of this ineffective habit, you might be pleasantly surprised to find in teachers a pool of talented professionals who are passionate about their subject matter and totally respectful of your dignity, self-worth and quest for empowerment.

Welcome teachers who, contrary to adultist scripts, seek nothing more than to help you discover your own source of motivation. The cruel adultist games which may have been played on you must not encourage you to continue playing games with yourself. Dig deep into your inner being. Find in that core what you want to become. Pursue those desires. An education is indispensable for that purpose. You must learn to trust teachers who clearly affirm you and applaud your quest.

The greatest achievement of any teacher is to guide a student into self-discovery. When that discovery explodes into reality and drives the student's search for purpose in life, then and only then does the promise of education really materialize. No teacher, no matter how gifted, talented, glib, informed or wise, can educate a student without the student giving the teacher permission to guide.

On the other hand, no student can become educated without the modeling, mentoring, technical assistance and guidance of teachers, as caring adults. If you are to succeed in your climb to the head of the class, you must stop rejecting teachers just because they are adults. Adults don't want to be disrespected any more than you do on the basis of age. "Olderism" cannot be replaced by "youngerism."

Lastly, the more of a troublemaker you become, the less educational progress you will make. The less educational progress you make, the more dependent you become on the adultist household you may be in. You will have less autonomy. You will earn less income.

So what's to be done? Get an education. Increase your autonomy. Learn to develop your sensitivity in the classroom so you won't make it a profession to knock heads with authority reps, such as those in the criminal justice system, later on. Don't sabotage the very process which can help you escape from adultists.

Think about your behavior and its impact. If you are a predator in the classroom, change your ways. Seek guidance. Go to a counselor and tell him or her that you are out of control and you want to change; that you want to become a willing learner, not a hostage in school; that you want to climb to the top of the class.

If you are not a defiant student, keep up the good work. You are a true blessing, especially if you have been influenced by adultists yet maintain a positive vision about education and demonstrate respect for teachers. Embrace the future by becoming an asset in helping to solve urgent problems. Become part of the solution instead of part of the problems of life. Get it? Then do it. Now. Take a giant step up to the head of the class.

My Personal Commitment

I, _____ , have identified three
practices describing my habit of Viewing Teachers as Adultists
which keep me from climbing to the head of the class.

1) _____

2) _____

3) _____

I will stop these behaviors in the following ways:

1) _____

2) _____

3) _____

I will invite the following three people to be my accountability
partners to help me climb to the head of the class.

1) _____ X. _____

2) _____ X. _____

3) _____ X. _____

Ask your accountability partners to sign their names.

X. _____ _____

      Your Signature   Date

Then...

...apply the ABCs of personal accountability by:

A   **Adjusting your behavior**

B   **Building on your progress**

C   **Continuing your collaboration**

Lasting Thoughts

"Adultism is the process of any person oppressing a younger person by using his/her age to wield authority. Perhaps olderism is a more accurate word since a 4-year-old can be adultist to a 2-year-old."

-Sheila Rose

"A child cannot be taught by someone who despises him."

-James Baldwin

"It's so hard when I have to and so easy when I want to."

-Sondra Anice Barnes

"Make sure you visualize what you really want, not what someone else wants for you."

-Jerry Gillies

"You will live your life secure in that you are no longer manipulated by what other people want you to do and be, but are directed by your own inner desires."

-H. Stanley Judd

"You may have a fresh start any moment you choose, for this thing we call 'failure' is not the falling down, but the staying down."

-Mary Pickford

Step

8

**Stop Seeking Solutions
Without Education**

Lessons from the Literature

"An education may do many things for you, if you are made of the right stuff, for you cannot fasten a two-thousand dollar education to a fifty-cent boy. The fool, the dude, and the shirk come out of school still not knowing anything, and they actually come out of the school pretty much as they went in. They dive deep in the Pierian Springs (whoever quaffed of these waters were supposed to be inspired by the Muses). As the duck who lives in the pond, they come up dry as the duck does. The school will not do anything for you if you do not wish to do something for yourself; but a well-spent life in school is one of the greatest helps to all good things."

-*Marva Collins*, Ordinary Children, Extraordinary Teachers

"If we put the emphasis upon the right things, if we live the life that is worthwhile, and then fail, we will survive all disasters, we will outlive all misfortune. We should be so well balanced and symmetrical, that nothing which could ever happen could throw us off our center, so that no matter what misfortune should overtake us, there would still be a whole magnificent man or woman left after being stripped of everything else."

-*Orison Swett Marden in Wynn Davis (Ed.)*, The Best of Success

You Be the Judge

Place an X in the box which best describes your own situation for each of the following 10 statements.

Seldom True	Often True	Most Often True	
❏	❏	❏	1. After high school, a job is what I really want.
❏	❏	❏	2. I have had it with school work, so after graduation I will never pick up another book.
❏	❏	❏	3. The only thing people need to get along in life is common sense.
❏	❏	❏	4. There is no connection between all the stuff I have to study and real life.
❏	❏	❏	5. Going to school is a waste of time because having a job that pays good money, a nice car, nice clothes and a few good friends is where it's at.
❏	❏	❏	6. Some of the biggest fools I know have gone to college and earned a bunch of degrees and diplomas, and are doing no better than I.
❏	❏	❏	7. My teachers make such a big deal about education, yet they are always complaining they do not make enough money.

❏ ❏ ❏ 8. I do not understand what the big deal is about education. If I am a fast learner and I can do the job, a certificate of graduation is not necessary.

❏ ❏ ❏ 9. I know people without education who have better paying jobs than people with degrees, which tells me that a lot of formal education is not needed.

❏ ❏ ❏ 10. If I thought that getting an education was really important to a successful future then I would study harder.

Subscores:

Column 1 subscore x 1 = _____

Column 2 subscore x 2 = _____

Column 3 subscore x 3 = _____

> Add all three subscores to get your total score.

Total Score: _____

If you scored:

10-15   Your perseverance is paying off. Continue your climb to the head of the class.

16-20   Caution! You are clearly slipping. Danger signs are showing. You need to take deliberate steps to change direction.

21-25   Stop seeking solutions without education! You are falling. Turn around quickly and start your climb back up.

26-30   You have crashed! Seek help immediately. While you may have hit the bottom, there is nowhere to go but up. This chapter is most definitely for you. Make a personal commitment now.

The Habit:
Seeking Solutions Without Education

*"No one wants a good education.
Everyone wants a good degree."*

-Lee Rudolph

Education is not everything. Earning diplomas and degrees is not a panacea for the world's problems. Graduating from high school and college are not magic feathers. It is irresponsible to preach otherwise.

Some people with college degrees and lots of letters after their names, graduates from very prestigious institutions, have failed miserably to make their lives count for something. The reverse is also true. Many people without much formal education have exercised leadership in making good things happen for themselves and others.

While education does not constitute the only answer to urgent and growing problems, it is valid to say that attempting to solve problems without an educated perspective is equivalent to cooking without utensils. No problem or meaningful challenge confronting our generation and those who will provide leadership in the 21st century can be successfully addressed without education. Education provides a framework by which to weigh options, seek comparisons, generate creative energy, apply scientific principles, discover patterns, test hypotheses and create concepts and theories useful in solving problems so we can improve the quality of our lives.

You must avoid seeking solutions to the challenges of life without an education. Love of learning is the educational agenda worth pursuing. The triumph of an educated spirit is reflected in self-initiated encounters with the world of ideas stored in books, videos, recordings, TV programs, museums, dialogue, meditation, group exercises, teamwork, study groups, travel, experiments and the arts. A thoughtful, critical assessment of how to apply lessons learned to the adventure of strengthening our society is second nature to an educated spirit.

Be aware that there are people without formal education in the mean streets selling drugs as well as people with degrees in high positions making compromises and betraying the public trust. A drug dealer will make more money than an educator. But making junkies of 13-year olds, feeding the drug habits of others, contributing to addicts' obsession with a leave of absence from reality – these are criminal. Making money from such activities demeans the human condition. Whether the drugs are legal or illegal, money earned through exploitation is dirty and contributes to human suffering.

Yes, the profits are huge. The roll of bills can be large enough to inspire awe on the part of poor, uneducated

122

youth as well as underpaid, hard working professionals. But can that kind of life help you to love and be loved? Can it help you feel secure, knowing that you are a caring member of a real family whose success is based on playing by the rules? That type of serenity cannot be purchased by a drug dealer's money.

A jail term hanging over your head, dying young in a bloody, violent confrontation, betrayed by a member of an illicit, inner circle – these are the life scripts of those who thrive on providing illegal poison to other human beings. That is why you must not be taken by fools who peddle poison instead of hope. Rather, opt for life scripts based on real values and meaningful activity. When you do this, you show insight and discernment and you're on your way to the head of the class.

People who achieve positions of power with the benefit of degrees and smarts can also do very destructive things. They are known as white-collar criminals. Former President Richard Nixon is a case in point. Ultimately, he was embarrassed and forced to resign from the presidency. The public trust was betrayed. His place in history was tarnished. His crime brought shame to the United States of America.

One great lesson from this debacle is that degrees and prestigious positions do not necessarily mean that a person is "educated." There is a difference between being schooled and being universalized through education. Being truly educated demands responsibility and honesty.

Knowing the history of what happened to President Nixon, and even fully appreciating the leadership he demonstrated in strengthening the relationship between the United States and China, one can learn the lesson of power misused. Through reading and analysis, a student is able to understand the good that can come out of achieving a high position of responsibility as well as the pitfalls of the abuse of power and trust.

People with or without formal education can choose a wrong path. Wynn Davis summarizes it well. He states:

The shortsighted embark on the dishonest path; the wise on the honest. For the wise know the truth: in helping others we help ourselves; and in hurting others we hurt ourselves. Character overshadows money, and trust rises above fame.

It is my hope that you will choose the path which helps rather than hurts others and yourself. You stand the best chance of helping others as an educated person. That means much more than completing a formal program of study.

Attending school, completing course requirements and receiving a certificate of completion do not necessarily mean that you have been educated. It could mean that you have simply been schooled. To be educated requires a willingness on your part, as a student, to be guided into the world of the profound. You must ponder, reflect and apply lessons learned to efforts at adding value to your talents. You must consciously and deliberately cooperate with adults, mentors, compassionate parents as well as other serious students to develop partnerships which enable you to embrace the demanding discipline of self-control and sacrifice. Cultivation of talent requires nothing less.

You must start viewing libraries as places for reading, not resting. Redefine your hours between classes as opportune times to review, clarify and update assignments and notes. Your definition of "homework" may have to change. Instead of thinking that "homework" relates to written assignments due the next day, it must take into consideration all work due in the future – a research paper, an upcoming examination perhaps weeks away – which require time on task today.

As a person interested in becoming universalized, simply meeting the legal requirements of attending school and doing minimal work just to get by will not do. Make time for work that will help you progress in projects which cultivate your talents. This is the only way to get to the head of the class. An education is not a destination, it is a journey. I cannot state often enough that the ultimate lesson from this journey is to learn how to learn. Too many students want the degree but care less about getting a good education in the process. You must not be one of these students.

You must value life, nature and human endeavors which lessen pain, promote healing, inspire laughter, remove barriers, discover truth and reduce prejudice, poverty and despair. This type of life celebrates differences and embraces identities which respect self and others. In contributing to quality relationships between people, you contribute to a global vision, transforming yourself into a citizen of the world through education. You must dare to imagine a universalized sense of self and then move to pursue education which can actualize your best hopes.

Without an education, the riddles of life cannot be solved. Every honest effort at seeking solutions to the problems of life requires an education. Earning diplomas and pursuing degrees provide wider options to becoming more valuable to society.

Someone once said that change is inevitable but growth is optional. To grow from every challenge and circumstance that a student may confront in life requires education. It means loving reading, expanding one's horizon and gaining breadth and depth by participating in forums where options are examined by others equally committed to the educational goal of becoming truly universalized.

It means traveling with informed companions who seek to make the world safer for differences. It means knowing how to temper earning money with the talent to make investments of time, resources and generosity to worthwhile causes. We must repair breaches between groups and work to make our world a better place for tomorrow.

In our increasingly complex society and shrinking world, in an Information Age where globalization has become an accepted reality, a formal education has gone from being the luxury of the elite to a necessity for all. Bearing in mind that education is not the answer to every problem, you must never forget that every problem, in order to be solved, benefits from education.

My Personal Commitment

I, _____ , have identified three
practices describing my habit of Seeking Solutions Without
Education which keep me from climbing to the head of the class.

1) _____

2) _____

3) _____

I will stop these behaviors in the following ways:

1) _____

2) _____

3) _____

I will invite the following three people to be my accountability
partners to help me climb to the head of the class.

1) _____ X. _____

2) _____ X. _____

3) _____ X. _____

Ask your accountability partners to sign their names.

X. _____ _____
      Your Signature   Date

Then...

...apply the ABCs of personal accountability by:

A **Adjusting your behavior**

B **Building on your progress**

C **Continuing your collaboration**

Lasting Thoughts

"Education is a social process... Education is growth... Education is not a preparation for life; education is life itself."

-John Dewey

"Badness you can get easily, in quantity: the road is smooth, and it lies close by. But in front of excellence the immortal gods have put sweat, and long and steep is the way to it."

-Hesiod

"Perhaps the most valuable result of all education is the ability to make yourself do the thing you have to do, when it ought to be done, whether you like it or not. It is the first lesson that ought to be learned."

-Thomas H. Huxley

"Am I willing to give up what I have in order to be what I am not yet? ... Am I able to follow the spirit of love into the desert? ... It is a frightening and sacred moment. There is no return. One's life is changed forever. It is the fire that gives us our shape."

-Mary Caroline Richards

" 'Would you tell me, please, which way I ought to go from here?'

'That depends a good deal on where you want to get to,' said the Cat.

'I don't much care where,' said Alice.

'Then it doesn't matter which way you go,' said the Cat."

-*Lewis Carroll*, Alice's Adventures in Wonderland

Step

9

Stop Pursuing Logical Paths to Wrong Destinations

Lessons from the Literature

"I was transferred into Sister Naomi's English class, and I vowed to be a model student. I managed to give oral book reports by asking one of the avid readers, usually a girl who spent her extra time in the library, about a book she had read. I'd remember the name of the book, stand up with cards in my hand, and proceed to tell the title, the author, the setting and the story. Somehow, in my warped logic, I didn't think this was cheating. I just thought I was defying a system that wouldn't or couldn't teach me."

-*John Corcoran*, The Teacher Who Couldn't Read

"It is not only what we do that determines the pattern of our lives, but also whom we choose to associate with. There are individuals who cannot tolerate solitude and must always surround themselves with other people. Such persons have a hard time acquiring complex skills or concentrating on difficult problems."

-*Mihaly Csikszentmihalyi, Kevin Rathunde, and Samuel Whalen*, Talented Teenagers

You Be the Judge

Place an X in the box which best describes your own situation for each of the following 10 statements.

Seldom True	Often True	Most Often True	
❏	❏	❏	1. I have been asked a question by a teacher in class only to be embarrassed by not having the answer because I chose to do something else rather than study.
❏	❏	❏	2. After getting lousy grades, I say I am going to do better and work harder but I do not walk the talk.
❏	❏	❏	3. I have chosen to do things which seemed more important than studying at the time, only to find out I was wrong in the end.
❏	❏	❏	4. If I decide to do something that is wrong, it is not hard for me to invent good reasons for doing it even though I know it will have a negative impact.
❏	❏	❏	5. I can easily convince my parents to let me put off things I should do so I can do something I want to do.
❏	❏	❏	6. My friends will, at times, persuade me to go along with them to activities when deep down I know I should be doing my schoolwork.

❏ ❏ ❏ 7. Watching a big television event has kept me from completing certain school tasks on time.

❏ ❏ ❏ 8. I use my computer and the Internet, but usually not for educational purposes.

❏ ❏ ❏ 9. I tell myself I will only play one video game only to end up losing hours of study time.

❏ ❏ ❏ 10. Knowing that my parents would not let me do something I wanted to do, I have lied to them.

Subscores:

Column 1 subscore x 1 = _____
Column 2 subscore x 2 = _____
Column 3 subscore x 3 = _____

> Add all three subscores to get your total score.

Total Score: _____

If you scored:

10-15 Your perseverance is paying off. Continue your climb to the head of the class.

16-20 Caution! You are clearly slipping. Danger signs are showing. You need to take deliberate steps to change direction.

21-25 Stop pursuing logical paths to wrong destinations! You are falling. Turn around quickly and start your climb back up.

26-30   You have crashed! Seek help immediately. While you may have hit the bottom, there is nowhere to go but up. This chapter is most definitely for you. Make a personal commitment now.

The Habit: Pursuing Logical Paths to Wrong Destinations

"Logic is the art of going wrong with confidence."

-Joseph Wood Krutch

When you act impulsively to satisfy a pressing need, chances are you'll come up with an intelligent and logical explanation to rationalize it. Doing this however – choosing immediate gratification and not looking beyond the urgent desires of the moment – can have disastrous consequences. Let me show you how.

Here is the contradiction. What is logical is not always correct. It may be sometimes, but not always. Academic failure could be a warning sign of this contradiction. Is it really possible to have smart, logical explanations for actions which promote academic failure? Yes!

A student once engaged me in a logical discussion regarding cars. He spoke of the merits of a new car over a used one. "Is it not true," he asked, "that when a person buys an old car he may be buying someone else's problems?" "Yes," I said. The answer seemed obvious. I didn't have to be a rocket scientist to figure that one out. He then proceeded to tell me that, to avoid making the disastrous mistake of buying someone else's problems, he was going to purchase a new car. His uncle would sign for the loan. Then he added, "I am taking a year off from my college studies."

"Oh, and why is that?" I countered. "Because I can't afford to pay for my new car and go to school at the same time," he concluded. It all seemed very reasonable. As far as he was concerned, because he did not want to buy someone else's problems, he had to abandon completing his academic program. Perhaps he did return to school, I don't know. He never communicated with me again. My hope is that he did.

The narrow question regarding the purchase of other people's problems was a set-up for me to agree with his logical argument that buying a new car was better than getting a used one. This student did not care to discuss other alternatives regarding his transportation predicament with me. We could have talked about possibilities like using public transportation, car pooling or exploring creative ways of buying a used car while minimizing the possibility of inheriting someone else's car problems – all possible while continuing his degree program. He focused on the purchase of a car as an issue not connected to any others. He failed to think critically.

The logical desire for the new car obscured complicated issues related to the consequences and impact of the decision. After all, cars are very expensive, especially if bought on credit where one is paying for the loan interest on top of the purchase price. Buying a city sticker, plates, an alarm, insurance plus a possible extended warranty – all these costs add up. Had he gotten a sound education, he would have been able to buy a car and much more. Think about it.

Here's another common way we follow logical paths to wrong destinations – Jokes! It is logical to laugh at a funny joke, especially if it's told to you with gusto and excellent timing, complete with gestures to maximize impact. Jokes also seem really funny when they target a group that's been stereotyped. These jokes release tension and promote an "us versus them" feeling. We get a good laugh at the expense of the targeted group.

The scripts we have about certain groups, who are consistently the butt of jokes, usually make the punch lines particularly delightful and memorable. So it is very logical that, every now and then, if you laugh out loud at a good joke, you will remember the scenario and will retell it to other peers. A good, funny joke becomes a priceless gem in the hands of a solid performer.

But you need to ponder the consequences of following the logical path of using debilitating humor about some groups, including your own, as a source of entertainment. Is humor which demeans, mocks and pokes fun at different groups a good, healthy way for you to climb to the top of the class? Think.

What is logical is not always correct. Building strong identity bonds with members of your own group at the expense of stigmatizing others may promote distrust and make you insensitive to people's feelings.

At this crucial time in our history, the need for unity based on an appreciation of diversity is most urgent. Laughter at the expense of people simply leads to a wrong destination. Don't go there. View others with respect. Team up with youth from different backgrounds to win championships. Reject hate acts, whether expressed in anger or humor. Join or start organizations in your school which promote understanding by reducing prejudice.

Work at seeking greater understanding, not more divisiveness. Exercise leadership in requesting class assignments that analyze and evaluate media programming which poison relationships between groups. Learn to laugh with others through healthy, uplifting and inclusive humor. Diversity is part of our collective legacy. Be a part of what helps to heal rather than what cheapens our dignity and humanity.

Romantic relationships and logic usually clash. This is another area where you might take logical paths to wrong destinations. By embarking on romantic relationships which use up a lot of your creative energy, time and resources that would otherwise be focused on achieving educational excellence, your journey to the head of the class might be frustrated. So please be alert. Learn to sit on your urges.

Becoming romantically entangled and sexually active is one path fraught with major dangers. The fear of pregnancy and disease, compounded by feelings of guilt and the worries which come with dealing with a complex relationship, make this path particularly burdensome. It is so exhausting and emotionally expensive! Having to lie and sneak around is also draining. Doing something which feels good may make sense in a world which promotes a "Just do it!" philosophy. But looming large on the walls of high school hallways are signs which cry out a warning that must be heeded, "If you go all the way, you won't get very far."

There are alternatives to the "Just do it" philosophy. Release pent up energy through sports, exercise and hard physical work. Socialize through group activities. Seek spiritual growth. Build a fierce determination to think, study and read. A person who leads a balanced life stands the best chance of resisting temptations of the flesh. To succeed in school, you must not be seduced by feelings of uncontrolled sexuality in need of immediate gratification.

It is easy to come up with logical reasons for quick fix and dangerous solutions. To quit or not to quit school in order to work, in hopes of returning to school later, is sometimes the question. There could be logical arguments in favor of such an interruption of your schooling.

Life may be intolerable where you are. You may need a place of your own. It takes money to put a deposit down on an apartment, pay rent and purchase the essentials so you think you have to quit school and go to work. The argument is compelling. Staying in school will simply not do. At least for the moment. Secure in the logic that such a step is necessary, you are prepared to take the plunge. It seems like the right thing to do. But is it?

Let's take a look at the destination you might reach as a result of following the logical path just outlined. Getting out of an intolerable situation may well lead you into an equally difficult or worse one. Paying your own way might be a bigger challenge than you think.

Working at jobs which pay wages commensurate with your worth in the marketplace may barely be enough to meet your new obligations. Wages after taxes, transportation, food and other expenses are paid for may fall short of your expectation. A lot of hidden costs related to health care and others may in fact leave you owing money rather than saving at the end of a pay period. So think about where you might be headed before you reason that leaving home is going to be better for you. In the long run, it might not be.

It could be better for you to stay put, continue your studies in school, and put up with a less than ideal setting until you are truly able to go out into a better tomorrow with your formal educational program completed.

It might be revealing to speak with people close to you who have interrupted their schooling. Find out how many returned as planned. Take notes, especially from those who thought of returning and did not do so. Ask them what they would do if they had a chance to do it again. You might be surprised at their insight born out of real life experience.

The desire to get out into the real world to gain perspective has a nice logical ring to it. When work competes with school, however, your commitment to education can falter. Summer jobs and part-time employment during the school year can provide some perspective on what working without completing a post-secondary program may feel like.

Use caution before you abandon the student mindset that is attuned to book learning, class discussion, study circles and academic projects. By joining the workforce, you may get used to being "free" from homework exercises, writing papers and preparing for examinations. This may influence you to become permanently distracted from the goal of pursuing formal education.

Leaving school and settling into a work schedule will connect you to new friendships with people not engaged in study. New social obligations will occupy your nights. Hanging out with friends, dating (with the added bonus of constant privacy since you will now have your own place) or watching videos will most likely replace study habits. Gone are the benefits of an education – the challenge of abstract thinking, chasing ideas, embracing concepts, organizing thought patterns, brainstorming with study partners, pursuing comparative frameworks of thought with passion, and revising drafts into clearer, sharper and more meaningful essays.

145

You must be very careful not to make the mistake of following logical paths to wrong destinations. Stay in school. Do your homework. Read, read and read. Continue to think critically. Grow in proficiency and sophistication. Do not procrastinate. Climb all the way to the top. Life will be better with an education under your belt. Don't fool yourself into interrupting your formal program of studies. Say yes to self-discipline.

Life is tough, even with an education. Without one, though, it will be much harder. Make it easier on yourself and the others who will depend on your good judgement today for their own journeys tomorrow.

Daily challenges will afford you opportunities to exercise wisdom on your journey to academic excellence. The series of small, even seemingly insignificant, decisions – the steps taken one way or the other, up or down – will ultimately determine whether the path you follow enriches or imprisons your spirit. So choose the path which leads upwards. The ineffective habit of not doing so will dull your senses into certain mediocrity. Your mind is too precious to waste. Protect it. It is your most valuable asset.

My Personal Commitment

I, _____ , have identified three
practices describing my habit of Pursuing Logical Paths to
Wrong Destinations which keep me from climbing to the head
of the class.

1) _____

2) _____

3) _____

I will stop these behaviors in the following ways:

1) _____

2) _____

3) _____

I will invite the following three people to be my accountability
partners to help me climb to the head of the class.

1) _____ X. _____

2) _____ X. _____

3) _____ X. _____

Ask your accountability partners to sign their names.

X. _____ _____
       Your Signature   Date

Then...

...apply the ABCs of personal accountability by:

A   **Adjusting your behavior**

B   **Building on your progress**

C   **Continuing your collaboration**

Lasting Thoughts

"It takes less time to do a thing right than to explain why you did it wrong."

-Henry Wadsworth Longfellow

"Even if you're on the right track, you'll get run over if you just sit there."

-Will Rogers

"If you set out to be liked, you would be prepared to compromise on anything at any time, and you would achieve nothing."

-Margaret Thatcher

"Do not follow where the path may lead. Go instead where there is no path and leave a trail."

-Muriel Strode

"Do not do what you would undo if caught."

-Leah Arendt

"The journey of a thousand miles begins with the first step."

-Chinese Proverb

Step 10

**Stop Failing to Look Up
by Not Getting Down**

Lessons from the Literature

"Some people are free to deviate because they risk very little if their deviant behavior is detected. But for others, the costs of detection far exceed the rewards of deviance... We tend to like and even love those to whom we are attached. The degree to which an individual is attached to others depends upon the number and closeness of his or her bonds: how much that individual cares about others (and is cared about in return) and, therefore, how much the person cares about what others think of his or her actions."
-Rodney Stark, Sociology

"She wanted all of her children to earn college degrees. No exceptions. If she had known I couldn't read or write, she would have realized her dream for me was pure fantasy. But exposure to my mother's high expectations must have inspired me. Because although I didn't believe I could do it, I did. I credit my mother for part of that achievement."
-John Corcoran, The Teacher Who Couldn't Read

You Be the Judge

Place an X in the box which best describes your own situation for each of the following 10 statements.

Seldom True	Often True	Most Often True	
❏	❏	❏	1. Even though I don't do as well as I should in school, my parents know that my love for them is strong and real.
❏	❏	❏	2. My parents, who love and sacrifice for me, work very hard to provide all the members of the family with our basic needs, but somehow I still can't get down to bringing home excellent grades.
❏	❏	❏	3. Because I am not getting good grades now, when I have my own family it will be necessary for other people to help my children with their homework.
❏	❏	❏	4. After reviewing my report card with my parents, I feel ashamed of my lack of progress and find myself hugging them and promising to do better.
❏	❏	❏	5. I have tried to keep my loved ones from finding out how poor some of my grades have been.
❏	❏	❏	6. I get tired of my parents telling me that if I truly loved them I must do better in my school performance.

☐   ☐   ☐   7. When school work becomes important to me I will get down to the business of working towards good grades but until then I wish all of my relatives would get off my back.

☐   ☐   ☐   8. Just because my parents didn't get a chance to finish school does not mean I have to sweat to get excellent grades to make them proud.

☐   ☐   ☐   9. While I do not do well in school all the time, I never forget a birthday or other significant holiday/event since I always bring gifts for the celebrations.

☐   ☐   ☐   10. I dream of earning the best grades and climbing to the head of the class to make my family proud, but my dreams are seldom realized.

Subscores:

Column 1 subscore x 1 = _____

Column 2 subscore x 2 = _____

Column 3 subscore x 3 = _____

> Add all three subscores to get your total score.

Total Score: _____

If you scored:

10-15   Your perseverance is paying off. Continue your climb to the head of the class.

16-20   Caution! You are clearly slipping. Danger signs are showing. You need to take deliberate steps to change direction.

21-25   Stop failing to look up by not getting down! You are falling. Turn around quickly and start your climb back up.

26-30   You have crashed! Seek help immediately. While you may have hit the bottom, there is nowhere to go but up. This chapter is most definitely for you. Make a personal commitment now.

The Habit:
Failing to Look Up by Not
Getting Down

"Education is a loan to be repaid with the gift of self."
-Lady Bird Johnson

When you look up to someone you admire and have affection for, then you've got to do whatever it takes to become a disciplined, motivated student headed straight to the top of the class. Your success in school is the best gift you can give them.

When you have someone you look up to, the challenge of getting down to the hard work of studying becomes less difficult. To love someone is to have the greatest motivation to adopt their values and meet their best hopes. A special bond between two people – between you, the student, and the person you love – can propel you to abandon laziness and become passionate about learning. It can inspire an eagerness to demonstrate that you are doing well in school.

As a student, the best response you can give to the caring, nurturing and loving people in your life is to succeed academically. No other gift can compare. Why? Because your success in school indicates a willingness to defer gratification, exercise self-control, follow directions, meet deadlines, grow autonomous and mature, become capable of networking with like-minded peers, and continue to develop and expand your knowledge. Above all else, you are headed in the right direction.

That fact creates joy in your loved ones. Your deliberate journey to the head of the class brings honor to those with their best hope in you. By striving to succeed in your course work, you inspire pride in the people who have invested in you. In a nutshell, you are getting down! In building a foundation through learning, you dramatically indicate that you really look up to those who love you.

When you succeed in school and become learned, you render honor to your parents, mentors, counselors and all the other wonderful people in your life who showed their love for you through hugs and kisses, celebrated your special days, boosted your spirits and cheered you on to success. By becoming educated, you show respect for positive family values. Your hard work, as evidenced by superior academic achievement, honors every sacrifice made by your parents. Your achievement is a credit to the wisdom of elders who alerted you to the pitfalls in life and how to avoid them.

Melba Patillo Beals was tempted to give up, to call it quits and stop living, in fact. Read her book, *Warriors Don't Cry*. Her grandmother is celebrated there for helping Melba in her journey to success:

During those days I felt so close to her, and I knew I had been silly for wanting to give up. Several times she looked at me and said, "Don't you know, child, how much I love you, how much your mama loves you? Whenever you think about going away from this earth, think about how you'd break my heart and your brother's heart. You might as well take your mother with you because she'd be beside herself."... She made me get a project I really liked and encouraged me to keep on top of it. I chose the blast-off of the Explorer, the satellite that put our country into the space race... Grandma studied up on the topic, and we talked for hours while she taught me how to do the quilting for Mother's birthday present.

The ultimate display of true loyalty to the values of those loving parents with the greatest hope in you is to enjoy and relish the task of climbing the very difficult steps to the head of the class. A person who gets down must face the challenges, the strain, the sweat and the pain leading to gains in academic achievement. The greatest high comes from the realization that you have taken control of your life and are engaged in supercharging your grades.

If it were possible to get all the love we wanted and needed as human beings without being held accountable by those whom we love, life would be easy. But life is not easy.

An educated person will experience growth by being able to cope with and, at times, even thrive on seemingly chaotic and painful experiences. To be able to do this, you must be enthused. A winner cannot be indifferent or passive. Someone wrote:

> *Indifference never wrote great works, nor thought out striking inventions, nor reared the solemn architecture that awes the soul, nor breathed sublime music, nor painted glorious pictures, nor undertook heroic philanthropies. All these grandeurs are born of enthusiasm and are done heartily.*

Universalize your spirit. Work hard to strengthen your cognitive skills and to nurture a love for aesthetic beauty. Foster an appreciation for music. Develop a passion for abstract formulas which can help you solve concrete problems.

Please continue to look up to grandparents, aunts and uncles, foster parents, good neighbors and teachers by getting down and doing your very best work in school. These understanding elders will be rewarded by your success. You must, therefore, respond positively to the challenge of discipline and hard work. Lazy study habits – ignoring deadlines, failing to think critically, refusing to build a powerful vocabulary through extensive reading, and not learning from the biographies of people who surmounted challenges and excelled – all these will seriously impede growth.

Younger sisters, brothers and other relatives may request technical assistance from you to complete a science project. They may request help in writing an essay or analyzing a literary work. If you did not take your own studies seriously before, would you have the knowledge and skills to help them? A lazy, non-productive student who fails to get down to the business of learning today may not be able to be valuable and loving to those dependent on him or her in the future. Mediocrity in school today will produce incompetent parents later who will have to tell their offspring that they cannot help them with their studies. Taking shortcuts today means failing to get down. So think about the future. Prepare to love your offspring.

So go for it! Don't stop. Love those who have their greatest hope in you by climbing to the top of the class. Your academic success will be the greatest act of reciprocity to those who love you.

My Personal Commitment

I, _____ , have identified three
practices describing my habit of Failing to Look Up by Not Getting
Down which keep me from climbing to the head of the class.

1) _____

2) _____

3) _____

I will stop these behaviors in the following ways:

1) _____

2) _____

3) _____

I will invite the following three people to be my accountability
partners to help me climb to the head of the class.

1) _____ X. _____

2) _____ X. _____

3) _____ X. _____

Ask your accountability partners to sign their names.

X. _____ _____
    Your Signature   Date

Then...

...apply the ABCs of personal accountability by:

A   Adjusting your behavior

B   Building on your progress

C   Continuing your collaboration

Lasting Thoughts

"We always love those who admire us; we do not always love those whom we admire."

-François de La Rochefoucauld

"Look at what you love on graduation day. Take the classes, the friends and the family that have inspired the most in you. Save them in your permanent memory and make a back-up disk. When you remember what you love, you will remember who you are. If you remember who you are, you can do anything."

-Cathy Guisewite

"Just don't give up trying to do what you really want to do. Where there is love and inspiration, I don't think you can go wrong."

-Ella Fitzgerald

"It is for us to pray not for tasks equal to our powers, but for powers equal to our tasks, to go forward with a great desire forever beating at the door of our hearts as we travel towards our distant goal."

-Helen Keller

"Jump into the middle of things, get your hands dirty, fall flat on your face, and then reach for the stars."

-Joan L. Curcio

Bibliography

Allstate Forum on Public Issues. *Labor Force 2000.*

Ashton-Warner, Sylvia. *Teacher.* New York, NY: Simon & Schuster, Inc., 1963.

Avi. *Nothing But the Truth.* New York, NY: Avon Books, 1991.

Bain, Josie G. and Joan L. Herman. *Making Schools Work for Underachieving Minority Students.* Westport, CT: Greenwood Press, 1990.

Ballantine, Jeanne H. *The Sociology of Education.* Englewood Cliffs, NJ: Prentice Hall, 1989.

Banks, James A. *Teaching Strategies for Ethnic Studies.* Newton, MA: Allyn and Bacon, Inc., 1987.

Bastian, Ann, Norm Fruchter, Marilyn Gittell, Colin Greer and Kenneth Haskins. *Choosing Equality.* San Francisco, CA: Public Media Center, 1985.

Baughman, M. Dale. *Baughman's Handbook of Humor in Education.* West Nyack, NY: Parker Publishing Company, Inc., 1974.

Beals, Melba Pattillo. *Warriors Don't Cry.* New York, NY: Washington Square Press, 1994.

Bierce, Ambrose. *The Devil's Dictionary*. Cleveland, OH: World Publishing Company, 1911.

Bigelow, Bill, Linda Christensen, Stan Karp, Barbara Miner and Bob Peterson. *Rethinking Our Classrooms*. Milwaukee, WI: Rethinking Schools, Ltd., 1994.

Bigler, Philip and Karen Lockard. *Failing Grades*. Arlington, VA: Vandamere Press, 1992.

Boocock, Sarane Spence. *Sociology of Education*. Boston, MA: Houghton Mifflin Company, 1980.

Boyko, Carrie and Kimberly Colen. *Hold Fast Your Dreams*. New York, NY: Scholastic Inc., 1996.

Brussell, Eugene E. *Webster's New World Dictionary of Quotable Definitions*. Englewood Cliffs, NJ: Prentice Hall, 1988.

Bullard, Sara. *Teaching Tolerance*. Publication Volume 2 Number 2 Montgomery, AL: Southern Poverty Law Center, 1993.

Bullard, Sara. *Teaching Tolerance*. Publication Volume 4 Number 1 Montgomery, AL: Southern Poverty Law Center, 1995.

Bunzel, John H. *Challenge to American Schools*. New
        York, NY: Oxford University Press, Inc., 1985.

Butler-Por, Nava. *Underachievers in School*. Chichester:
        John Wiley & Sons, 1987.

Canter, Lee with Marlene Canter. *Assertive Discipline for
        Parents*. New York, NY: Harper & Row,
        Publishers, Inc., 1982.

Castellanos, Diego. *The Best of Two Worlds*. Trenton,
        NJ: New Jersey State Department of Education,
        1983.

Charters, Gillian. *Education Alumni Bulletin*.
        Publication Vol. 308 Number 3 Cambridge, MA:
        Harvard Graduate School of Education, 1994.

Collins, Marva. *"Ordinary" Children, Extraordinary
        Teachers*. Norfolk, VA: Hampton Roads
        Publishing Company, Inc., 1992.

Corcoran, John with Carole C. Carlson. *The Teacher
        Who Couldn't Read*. Colorado Springs, CO:
        Focus on the Family, 1994.

Csikszentmihalyi, Mihaly, Kevin Rathunde and Samuel
        Whalen. *Talented Teenagers: The Roots of Success
        & Failure*. Cambridge, MA: Cambridge
        University Press, 1993

Davis, Wynn. *The Best of Success*. Lombard, IL: Great
    Quotations Publishing Company, 1988.

Delpit, Lisa. *Other People's Children*. New York, NY:
    New Press, 1995.

Droke, Maxwell. *The Speaker's Handbook of Humor*.
    New York, NY: Harper & Brothers Publishers,
    1956.

Duke, Benjamin. *The Japanese School*. New York, NY:
    Praeger Publishers, 1986.

Esar, Evan. *Dictionary of Humorous Quotations*. New
    York, NY: Paperback Library, Inc., 1966.

Foster, Herbert L. *Ribbin' Jivin' & Playing the Dozens*.
    Cambridge, MA: Ballinger Publishing Company,
    1986.

Fried, Jane and Associates. *Shifting Paradigms in Student
    Affairs*. Lanham, MD: University Press of
    America, Inc., 1995.

Gardner, Howard. *Multiple Intelligences*. New York, NY:
    BasicBooks, 1993.

Gartner, Bob. *High Performance Through Teamwork*.
    New York, NY: Rosen Publishing Group, Inc.,
    1996.

Ginott, Dr. Haim G. *Teacher & Child*. New York, NY: Avon Books, 1972.

Gollnick, Donna M. and Philip C. Chinn. *Multicultural Education in a Pluralistic Society*. St. Louis, MO: C.V. Mosby Company, 1983.

Goodlad, John I. *A Place Called School*. New York, NY: McGraw-Hill Book Company, 1984.

Greenstein, Jack. *What the Children Taught Me*. Chicago, IL: University of Chicago Press, 1983.

Greer, Colin. *The Great School Legend*. New York, NY: BasicBooks, 1972.

Grosjean, François. *Life with Two Languages*. Cambridge, MA: Harvard University Press, 1982.

Gross, Ronald. *The Teacher and the Taught*. New York, NY: Dell Publishing Co., Inc., 1963.

Haden Sr., Joseph. *Educational Pathways Magazine*. Publication Volume 1 Issue 2 Fort Washington, MD: Educational Pathways, 1997.

Holt, John. *What Do I Do Monday?*. New York, NY: Dell Publishing Co., Inc., 1970.

Johnson, Louanne. *School is Not a Four-Letter Word.* New York, NY: Hyperion, 1997.

Kozol, Jonathan. *Savage Inequalities.* New York, NY: HarperPerennial, 1991.

Krashen, Stephen. *The Power of Reading.* Englewood, CO: Libraries Unlimited, Inc., 1993.

Krogness, Mary Mercer. *Just Teach Me, Mrs. K.* Portsmouth, NH:Heinemann, 1995.

Kunjufu, Jawanza. *Motivating and Preparing Black Youth to Work.* Chicago, IL: African American Images, 1986.

Lattin, Vernon E., Rolando Hinojosa, and Gary D. Keller. *Tomás Rivera: The Man and His Work.* Tempe, AZ: Bilingual Review/Press, 1988.

Lerner, Michael and Cornel West. *Jews and Blacks.* New York, NY: G.P. Putnam's Sons, 1995.

Lightfoot, Sara Lawrence. *The Good High School.* New York, NY: Basic Books, Inc., 1983.

Linksman, Ricki. *Solving Your Child's Reading Problems.* New York, NY: Carol Publishing Group, 1995.

Meinberg, Dr. Sherry L. *Into the Hornet's Nest.* Saratoga, CA: R & E Publishers, 1993.

Miller, Mary Susan. *Save Our Schools*. San Francisco, CA: Harper San Francisco, 1993.

Moore, Joan and Harry Pachon. *Hispanics in the United States*. Englewood Cliffs, NJ: Prentice-Hall, Inc., 1985.

Morris, William. *The Clear and Simple Thesaurus Dictionary*. New York, NY: Grosset & Dunlap, 1971.

Nakanishi, Don T. and Tina Yamano Nishida. *The Asian American Educational Experience*. New York, NY: Routledge, 1995.

Payne, Dr. Ruby K. *Poverty: A Framework for Understanding and Working with Students and Adults from Poverty*. Baytown, TX: RFT Publishing, 1995.

Peterson, Art. *Teachers*. New York, NY: New American Library, 1985.

Pool, Harbison and Jane A. Page. *Beyond Tracking*. Bloomington, IN: Phi Delta Kappa Educational Foundation, 1995.

Ravitch, Diane. *The Schools We Deserve*. New York, NY: Basic Books, Inc., 1985.

Robb, Laura. *Whole Language Whole Learners*. New York, NY: William Morrow and Company, Inc., 1994.

Rosemond, John. *Ending the Homework Hassle*. Kansas City, MO: Andrews and McMeel, 1990.

Rosenthal, Nadine. *Speaking of Reading*. Portsmouth, NH: Heinemann, 1995.

Saal, Rollene. *The New York Public Library Guide to Reading Groups*. New York, NY: Crown Trade Paperbacks, 1995.

Sizer, Theodore R. *Horace's School*. New York, NY: Houghton Mifflin Company, 1992.

Sleeter, Christine E. *Empowerment through Multicultural Education*. Albany, NY: State University of New York Press, 1991.

Stark, Rodney. *Sociology*. Belmont, CA: Wadsworth Publishing Company, 1987.

Turner, Harry G. *You Can Do It!* Santa Monica, CA: Merritt Publishing, 1997.

Vail, Priscilla L. *Smart Kids with School Problems*. New York, NY: E.P. Dutton, 1987.

Walton, Priscilla H. *Multicultural Education*. Publication
Volume 3 Number 4 San Francisco, CA: Caddo
Gap Press, 1996.

Warner, Carolyn. *Treasury of Women's Quotations*.
Englewood Cliffs, NJ: Prentice Hall, 1992.

Weis, Lois. *Class, Race, & Gender in American
Education*. Albany, NY: State University of New
York Press, 1988.

Wexler, Philip. *Sociology of Education*. Publication Vol.
63 Number 1 New York, NY: Boyd Printing
Company., 1990.

Wexler, Philip. *Sociology of Education*. Publication Vol.
63 Number 3 New York, NY: Boyd Printing
Company., 1990.

Wood, Dr. George H. *Schools That Work*. New York,
NY: Penguin Group, 1992.

About the Author

Dr. Samuel Betances is an educator whose humor and insight make him a most sought after speaker, consultant and workshop facilitator. He not only survived poverty and dropping out of school but went on to earn a Masters and Doctorate at Harvard University. After working for the U.S. Office of Education and The National Institute of Education, he went on to teach for 23 years as a Professor of Sociology at Northeastern Illinois University. He now lectures throughout the world to public and private organizations interested in developing policies, programs and practices by which to embrace the challenge of change. His passion for youth, the promise of education, and sharing the lessons learned in his journey from Harlem to Harvard gives him the greatest satisfaction. Dr Betances lives in Chicago with his wife, Laura. He is the father of twin sons, David and Daniel, and their older sister, Cristina, who were all successful products of the Chicago Public Schools.

For more information on scheduling Dr. Samuel Betances for keynote addresses, workshop presentations and training programs please contact:

Souder, Betances and Associates, Inc.
Pacific Suite
5448 N. Kimball Ave.
Chicago, IL 60625-4620
Phone: (773) 463-6374
Fax: (773) 463-0429
E-mail: info@betances.com
Website: www.betances.com

Product Information

New Century Forum, Inc. is the publisher and distributor of Dr. Samuel Betances' audio and print products for the program *"Ten Steps to the Head of the Class"* for students and teachers.

For more information or to order, contact:

New Century Forum, Inc.
6348 N. Milwaukee Ave.
PMB 319
Chicago, IL 60646-3728
Phone: 888-45-FORUM (toll free)
         or 773-463-1667

United Learning, Inc. is currently the authorized distributor of Dr. Samuel Betances' video series on workforce diversity entitled, *"Harness the Rainbow"* and on urban education, *"Unity through Diversity."*

For more information or to order, contact:

AGC/United Learning
1560 Sherman Avenue, Suite 100
Evanston, IL 60201
Phone: 800-323-9084 (toll free)
Fax: 847-647-0918 or 847-328-6706
Website: http://www.unitedlearning.com

Quantity Purchases

Companies, schools, professional groups, clubs, and other organizations may qualify for special terms when ordering quantities of these products.